HANDBOOK FOR ART AND DESIGN

HANDBOOK FOR ART AND DESIGN

ROBIN JESSON
Head of the Faculty of Art and Design, Barnet College

Longman
Scientific &
Technical

Longman Scientific & Technical,
Longman Group UK Limited,
Longman House, Burnt Mill, Harlow,
Essex CM20 2JE, England
and Associated Companies throughout the world.

First published 1984
Third impression 1989
Second edition 1991

British Library Cataloguing in Publication Data
Jesson, Robin
 Handbook for art and design. – 2nd ed
 1. Great Britain Educational institutions. Curriculum
 Subjects: Arts
 I. Title II. Jesson, Robin, *Handbook for art and design students*
 700

Set in 10/11pt Linotron 202 Plantin
Produced by Longman Group (FE) Limited
Printed in Hong Kong

For Christopher and Kate

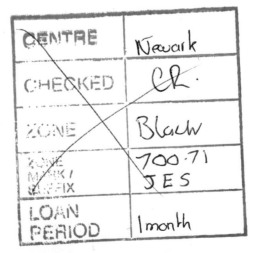

Contents

Acknowledgements

We are indebted to the following for permission to reproduce copyright material:
Council for National Academic Awards for extracts from *Directory of Degree & Diploma of Higher Education Courses* 1981–2; Kodak Ltd for Table & adapted extracts from pp 19, 6–8, 15 *Kodak Publication No AM2–1(H)*; Regional Advisory Council for Technological Education for adapted Table from p 102/3 *A Compendium of Advanced Courses in Colleges of Further & Higher* Education; Technician Educational Council for an extract from Section 3 *General Guidelines for Art & Design Studies* pub. Apr. 1979; the Victoria and Albert Museum for our Figs. 1.6, 1.7, 1.8, 1.9 and 1.12; Peter Blake for our Fig. 1.11; the Institute of Agricultural History and Museum of English Rural Life for our Fig. 3.2; Ironbridge Gorge Museum Trust for our Fig. 3.5; Principal, Barnet College for our Figs. 1, 1.1, 1.10, 2.3, 2.4, 3.1, 3.3(a), 3.3(b), and 3.4.

Special thanks are due to the many artists, designers, lecturers, students, friends, manufacturers and suppliers, past and present, who have made contributions to this book with expert advice on the specialist areas.

Preface to the Second Edition

Since its first publication in 1984 the readership of this handbook has widened and for this edition the book has been re-titled *Handbook for Art and Design*.

All sections have been revised and updated. Students will find information to help them identify courses and make a choice of a specialist subject. For the general reader it remains a basic guide to the whole range of creative art and design activities.

Where an asterisk appears please refer to the glossary for an explanation of the term used.

Introduction

You should be able to pick up a piece of wood and find you have a bird in your hand.

Pablo Picasso

This is a reference book and consumer guide for the beginner. It contains basic information on the nature of various creative activities, materials, equipment, research facilities, college courses and career prospects.

Many art and design activities such as ceramics, jewellery, photography, weaving, print-making, machine-knitting, fashion design and textile design and printing can be inexpensively carried out by beginners with the minimum of facilities. Full-time and part-time courses in departments, faculties and colleges of art and design provide access to more sophisticated resources and to teaching by professional artists and designers.

The practice of art and design involves the development of perceptual, conceptual, intuitive, imaginative and analytical abilities involving problem-solving; a knowledge and understanding of social, historical and environmental influences; skill acquisition; the learning of a specialised vocabulary and the development of individual talents.

CREATIVITY

At the beginning of all creative work the individual response to a given situation is all that exists. It is this response that stimulates in the creative personality the activities that follow. It can be nurtured and cultivated, but it is almost impossible to teach and cannot be learnt by reading a book. The only practical method is to attempt creative work.

Some people are inhibited from trying to learn a craft or involving themselves in creative activities because they believe that they cannot draw. In fact, most people from an early age can make marks on a surface which quite clearly represent their view of the visible world or that of their imagination. What concerns them, however, is their belief, usually gained as they approach adult life, that they cannot draw when comparing their efforts with the drawing abilities of those they admire. Everyone can draw, but some can more easily communicate by drawing than in other ways such as by the written word, music or speech. What is communicated is more important than how it is communicated. It is possible to train someone to observe and record visual observations. This involves a process of selection, from all the data available, of the most important elements. This selection process is unique for each person and it is the quality of what is communicated that determines whether or not the selection has been appropriate.

DEVELOPMENT OF IDEAS

Everyone concerned with the creative process has to start with an idea that can be developed, usually progressively, until the potential of the original idea is exhausted. This ability to develop an idea beyond the initial stages is crucial to the development of the artist and designer. The inherent possibilities contained within the original thought must be discovered, drawn out, explored and experimented with, using a range of materials. Without this development only repetition can follow; tired, outworn cliches which lack creative vitality. A simple example will help to explain some possibilities for the development of ideas.

An observation of the changing effects of light on a group of objects can start with a series of monochrome studies, perhaps in pencil, develop into tonal studies in colour and lead to work in a variety of media, possibly including photography, print-making and designs carried out in clay, metal, wood, plaster, plastics or mixed media materials. The idea could be developed into a print for textiles or for a fashion fabric, used as the basis for film animation or treated as a surface pattern on domestic tableware or household linens. This exploratory method is also a means of self-discovery, testing the individual's capability to respond to a particular problem and to exhaust all the possibilities. It is not necessary to have expensive and sophisticated tools in order to make worthwhile images. In fact, primitive tools often liberate the creative senses in unexpected ways. It is also a common experience to find that accidents or unintentional developments can be used creatively.

CONVENTIONS

Art and design have well-established conventions. A drawing such as that by the student shown in Fig. 1 uses such a convention. The model

---

Fig. 1   *Life drawing by Foundation Course student, Faculty of Art and Design – Barnet College*

drawn by the student was not surrounded by a line; and a photograph of the same model would have quite a different appearance. The idea that a drawn line can represent what is actually seen in the visual world as solid form, or even that a drawing in black and white can convey the form and character of a person whose real existence is in colour is widely understood and accepted. Because artistic conventions are so well established it is possible to communicate complex and sophisticated ideas in simple and direct ways.

Another means of communication by convention is the symbol. Information signs are an example of complex instructions being conveyed in a manner which is direct and immediately intelligible. Symbols can be understood internationally and easily overcome language barriers. It is not necessary to know any language to find the way to the toilets at an airport. The stylised male and female figures shown on the signs are immediately understood, even by very small children. The map of the London Underground system is a brilliant example of a complex railway system explained in readily understandable symbolic terms. In that the designer has combined colour, signs and the names of stations to explain complex links between different lines, connections to main railway stations and the sequence of stations on each line without directly referring to the actual geography of the area.

VOCABULARY

Studying for any activity, whether as a potential professional or as an amateur, requires a basic knowledge of the vocabulary used by the practitioners. All professions have a particular way of using language, a jargon, and artists and designers use some words in ways which are not common to their meaning in everyday life. Words such as form, line, tone, mass, structure and volume also have uses in other art forms such as music and architecture. In order to communicate effectively with others it is necessary to understand this vocabulary and in order to aid understanding a glossary is included at the end of the book. Words that appear in the glossary are signalled in the text by an asterisk.

TECHNOLOGY

Rapid technological developments are affecting the work of designers as they also affect other aspects of work in general. The use of microprocessors★ as design tools, the development of 'dry' camera systems, holograms★ and lasers★, the use of computers for the production processes in the fashion and textile industries and the draughting capabilities of the new technology mean that young designers looking forward to a working life in art and design must be prepared to adjust and rethink the use of the tools by which creative expression is made tangible.

STYLE

Everyone sees the visual world in a different way, although individual reactions are conditioned by cultural conventions.

Avoiding a stereotyped response to a creative problem is essential. Simply repeating what was originally developed by, for example, the Art Nouveau* movement is negative. Rediscovery has a place in creativity, but it cannot be done in the terms of the past. Developments in the visual arts have parallels in literature, music, architecture and philosophical ideas, and an appreciation of these links can add new dimensions to individual responses to contemporary life. Such relationships can more easily be appreciated by a study of the past. Not all the characteristics of a particular period will come together at the same time in the same place. The style of a period is a product of action and reaction on the part of creative people and the speed by which such information is spread. The present rate of technological change and the fast dissemination of information now means that an awareness of stylistic change is rapidly spread world-wide by very large numbers of people, an international style. The time-gap between the development of an idea and its assimilation into the broader area of style can now be just a few months. This particularly applies to the more ephemeral arts: fashion, graphic design, television, film and photography. Economics can also have an effect on style. This development of new materials with significant cost savings can be reflected in the style of furniture or the manufacture of carpets or textiles. The speeding up of the information process can lead to a retreat from the contemporary scene into the styles of the past, such as Victoriana or the period of the 1920s and 1930s. The speed of change, with its economic implications, can inhibit people from living directly within their own time in terms of style. It is expensive to maintain a life style rapidly adapting to stylistic changes and a retreat into the past is an easy escape. Some people possibly consider it better to be completely out of date than always just out of date, and it is often fashionable to live in the style of the past rather than the present.

Finding the best means for developing creative ideas and the kind of support that is available is the aim of this book. Some of the illustrations are by young art and design students at the start of their professional careers. All the recommendations for materials and equipment are based on the practical experience of artists and designers who are also teachers.

5

Note

This Handbook contains references to materials and equipment from a number of manufacturers and agents. While every effort has been made to ensure that the products mentioned are available, readers are advised to check with their local suppliers as some items may be withdrawn and manufacturers are continually improving and modifying their products.

General art and design

1.1 DRAWING

Drawing is a fundamental art and design activity concerned with the visual recording of observations, the expression of concepts in visual terms and image-making.

Experience will ensure the choice of the most suitable drawing implement for the image required. It is essential to experiment with different tools and to avoid developing techniques that can inhibit the individuality of image-making. Be prepared to be surprised by some of the images made and to see them as personal ways of communication.

Drawing systems are ways of visually explaining complex ideas to other people.

1.2 DRAWING MATERIALS

Charcoal

The best drawing charcoal is specially prepared for artists and designers. One of the best charcoals to use is in the Pitt range of artists' materials. It is made in five grades, extra soft, soft, medium, hard and extra hard and is round in shape. Rowney make a charcoal pencil, medium grade, which is a useful addition to life-drawing materials. The Criterium Clutch Pencil is suitable for 5–6 mm diameter leads of charcoal. The removable tip is fitted with a sharpener and supplied with a length of Conte compressed charcoal.

Crayons

It is sometimes difficult to manage the whole range of colours and tones of crayons until familiar with their characteristics. The type of working surface is very important. Normally avoid shiny, smooth surfaces which cannot give the crayon enough bite to work at its best. Gain experience with crayons of one colour in a range of tones before buying a number of different colours. Explore the water-resistant wax or oil qualities of some crayons. Use them with other mediums such as drawing inks or acrylic colours.

Crayons are available in a number of forms including crayon pencils, square and round section, water-resistant and water-soluble. One of the largest ranges is made by the Swiss manufacturer Caran D'Ache. Their range is available with a choice of 84 colours. Neo-color 1 is water-resistant. Neo-color 2 is water-soluble.

Crayons are suitable for use on a wide range of materials and are light-resistant. It is advisable to use crayons in a special holder as this allows the utilisation of the whole length of the crayon and helps to keep the artwork free of unwanted smudges. Neo-color 1 crayons are soluble in white spirit or turpentine and, when soluble, can be used with a brush. They can be erased by gently scraping the surface with a knife or scalpel.

Another firm that provides an interesting range of crayons is Berol. They offer three main types which are useful, including a chunky, round-section crayon called Cascade and a plastic-sheathed stick of solid colour called Verithik which can be resharpened. The colour range of both types, however, is limited. Berol's Artworker square-section crayon is, however, available in fifteen colours including black and white.

The Pitt range is ideal for life drawing. These crayons are made in black (medium and soft), white, sanguine and sepia (medium) in square sections. They also make a set of grey crayons, two each of six shades, and a set of brown crayons with twelve different assorted brown shades. One advantage of using a limited range of colours and tones is the opportunity to make contrasts by tone alone, without changing the colour.

Conte crayons are very popular. They are made in black – No. 1 medium (HB); No. 2 soft (B); and No. 3 extra soft (BB) – sepia, bistre and red sanguine in one degree only.

Erasers

Erasers can be the curse of drawing. The first inclination of many beginners is to produce a 'work of art' and this often involves rubbing out any marks that fail to achieve the desired effect.

The time could be more profitably used by actually drawing. A study of the drawings of famous artists will often show that all their errors of observation have not been erased but left as a record alongside the finished work. This particularly applies when the artists are of the stature of Leonardo or Michelangelo.

Erasers, however, have their place and for some work, where preliminary stages have to be removed, they are essential.

There are special erasers available for a number of specific tasks. The most useful types are as follows:

Plastic (kneaded putty rubber). This can be shaped, is non-abrasive and suitable for soft graphite, charcoal and pastel work.

Gum (art gum). Free of grease, soft and pliable, but crumbles so can be messy to use. Cheese-like in texture.

Blaisdell (paper covered – pencil shaped). For erasing detail. Eraser-sticks for Indian ink and ballpoint.

Ink eraser. Very hard and abrasive. Will easily scratch paper surfaces.

Plastic (vinyl). Hard – does not crumble.

Fibreglass. For very difficult erasing. Pencil or cigar shaped. Ideal for Indian ink erasing.

Erasing knives. Similar in design to a scalpel, with a specially designed blade.

For removing feltmarker inks from artwork or clothing the Edding Thinner V100 may be useful. Always experiment first on a small unimportant sample. It will not work on PVC (polyvinyl chloride). Ordinary ink marks can sometimes be removed with methylated spirit.

A useful drafting eraser is the Mars 527–30, a white vinyl eraser which comes in a pencil-shaped holder.

For erasing type or print use Tipp-Ex or a similar correction fluid. Liquid erasers sometimes need dilution with an approved solvent to maintain the flow.

Partial erasing or highlighting of texts can be effectively done with a suitable highlighter such as the Staedtler top-marker which is available in six colours.

All major manufacturers offer ranges of erasers. The Edding range is particularly useful for design students.

Feltmarkers

Feltmarkers normally consist of a barrel-shaped ink container, often short and chunky in appearance, with a felt top providing a stroke width from about 0.3 mm to 2.0 mm. Some manufacturers offer refillable markers and replacement felts. The colour range of Magic Markers is 123 colours including eighteen shades of grey. Feltmarkers have some limitations for drawing, mainly due to their squat shape and the nature of the felt tip, but they are widely used by graphic designers for 'roughs', i.e. preliminary layouts.

Tips are usually chamfered, pointed, square or rectangular. Markers are available for all types of surfaces including metal, stone and wood.

The range of inks include permanent, lightfast, waterproof, opaque and water-soluble types.

The Berol range includes a refillable marker with three interchangeable nibs and a specially developed valve which acts to stop evaporation, a problem with these markers when they are not in use.

They also market a double-ended marker in their Karisma range. This marker has two separate tips, one at each end giving the choice of a thick or thin tip. There are 116 colours in this range.

One of the largest specialist ranges is provided by C. W. Edding who were pioneers in this field. They produce seventeen different types of feltmarker ranging from those designed for drawing on unusual surfaces such as plastic foils to three made for use as writing instruments. The Edding 750 with a range of five colours, black, red, blue, green and yellow, is a good basic feltmarker for general use.

Fibrepens

Fibrepens offer more control than feltmarkers as they are usually longer in shape and the fibre tips are capable of detailed work. The stroke width varies from 0.3 mm to 3 mm, but also includes tips capable of being used as fine brushes. The tips can vary from firm to supple. The fibrepen colour range is large. Rechargeable cartridges are made for some models.

Fibrepens are widely used, particularly in design studios and for fashion illustration.

Always purchase pens from a specialist retailer if possible. Edding offer 21 different types of fibrepens for a variety of purposes. The Staedtler Lumocolor range is designed for overhead-projector work. This range is available in both non-permanent (water-soluble) and permanent (solvent-based) types.

The Edding 1340 series brushpen is very popular and is available in twelve colours; but the three primary colours plus black would be a useful start to a collection.

Fixatives

All work that is likely to smudge or rub off needs spraying with a lacquer fixative. It is possible to buy a small mouth spray diffuser and a bottle of fixative solution quite cheaply, but the most effective method is to use an aerosol fixative. Follow the manufacturer's instructions carefully. It is often necessary to work in a well-ventilated space as the fumes from the lacquer can cause distress. Fixatives are transparent and should not affect the appearance of the work.

Graphite sticks

Solid sticks of graphite without a wood, pencil-like casing. They can be sharpened like a pencil. Very useful for life drawing, they are made in four degrees of hardness, HB, 3B, 6B and 9B by Faber-Castell.

Lead holders

A useful alternative to the pencil is the lead holder containing drawing lead. Holders are also sometimes known as automatic pencils and their main advantage is the ready availability of the lead for a period of continuous drawing. A wide range of holders is available and the prices vary considerably. For beginners a simple holder is quite suitable, but the more advanced holders have an almost indefinite life and are elegant, well-designed additions to a set of drawing tools. Remember that a different holder will be needed for each line width of lead, but one holder can contain leads of different degrees of hardness.

The majority of holders provide an automatic feed system which keeps the lead always available for drawing. Line widths range from 0.3 mm to 3.0 mm. The width is usually identified on the holder. Some makes include a cleaning needle and an eraser.

The Caran D'Ache Fixpencil range is useful for all types of drawing. The Edding P3 is made in three diameter sizes, 0.5 mm, 0.7 mm and 0.9 mm, with a choice of seven degrees of hardness. Berol make a range of four types of holder, of which the Turquoise 10 is especially designed for draughtsmen, and Faber-Castell have an excellent range called the TK with fully automatic lead feed available on the TK-Matic. The Mars range from Staedtler is also very popular. This firm makes an inexpensive fineline lead holder (0.5 mm only) called the 775 Micro F and a larger diameter 2 mm lead holder called the 785 Mars Technico. For information about leads see page 13.

Inks

Drawing inks of all kinds are widely used. The traditional Indian ink is excellent for work being prepared for reproduction and the small bottles of coloured drawing inks have many uses in the studio. They can be used with pen or brush or used in combination with Indian ink. A little ink goes a long way so only initially buy in small quantities. Brushes and pens should be thoroughly cleaned after use.

Drawing inks are useful when used with other drawing materials. Explore their water-soluble characteristics by using them with wax or oil crayons. Their staining possibilities should also be explored.

There are a wide range of ink cartridges made for refillable pens of all kinds. Jars or pots of refill inks are also useful for some feltmarkers and similar tools with a large ink storage capacity. Feltmarkers that have dried up can sometimes be used again by using an appropriate thinner such as the Edding V100. Most inks can be sprayed or used with an airbrush.

Indian inks

Pitch black, fast drying, waterproof. Available in a range of sizes from a number of manufacturers.

Drawing inks

Water-resistant and waterproof when dry. These inks are intermixable and can usually be diluted with distilled water. They dry quickly but are vulnerable to light, and therefore work needs protection if the colours are not to fade. A good colour range is available. Winsor & Newton stock a range of 20 colours, together with black and white. They also have gold and silver non-waterproof inks. Rowney also has a range of 20 colours, including black, silver and gold.

Choose about six colours for a start: Lemon yellow; Vermilion; French ultramarine; Brown; Black; White.

Drawing inks can be used with pens and water-colour brushes.

Instruments

Work in technical illustration, graphic design, interior design, exhibition design or other aspects of three-dimensional design may require a set of drawing instruments. Some students will already have instruments purchased while at school and in many cases these will be suitable for the early stages of college courses. Students should consult their tutors before purchasing any new instruments.

Precision drawing instruments can be very expensive as they are made for work of a highly skilled nature. Most manufacturers offer a student range of compass sets such as the Faber-Castell 174370 which includes a divider and compass with pencil and pen inserts. An adjustable triangle, set square, protractor and rule may be needed to complete a basic kit which can be extended as the need arises.

Rulers

Purchase a good-quality rule. Ideally this should show both imperial and metric graduation. Wood rules usually last longer than plastic. A long steel rule for use with a knife when cutting card is very useful, particularly when mounting completed work. A rule approximately 60 cm long is ideal for this type of work.

Knives

A basic cutting tool is essential for a variety of tasks. The most familiar type is probably the Stanley knife with a set of interchangeable blades. Other makes include the Edding M18 cutter and the UNO Neatrim multipurpose cutter which is shaped like a pen and has a retractable blade. The cutter fits Swann Morton blades and also has a removable end for accessory storage. Surgical scalpels can also be useful general cutting tools. Buy a knife that is capable of easily cutting through thick mounting card and preferably one with interchangeable blades.

All knives can be dangerous if used incorrectly and many minor accidents to fingers occur when work in the studio has to be mounted.

Never draw the blade towards the body and always use a suitable support underneath the work to avoid cutting other surfaces, and a safety straight edge such as that supplied by Daler-Rowney.

Palette knives/Painting knives

These knives are available in steel and stainless steel. The straight-blade knives range in length from about 75 mm to 130 mm (3 in. to 5 in.). The trowel knives are made in a range of shapes including a diamond, pear and trowel. For work with acrylic or polymer paints a stainless-steel knife is essential. Use a knife to mix the paint on the palette and to apply paint when an impasto (thick laying on of pigments) is required. Beginners can usually manage with one straight blade and one trowel.

Leads

All leads have to be used with some type of lead holder (see page 10). They are graded by line width and hardness. Line widths range from 0.3 mm to 3 mm. Leads are available in black and ranges of up to 21 colours for use on a variety of surfaces.

There are two main types of leads: graphite, which is a mixture of graphite and clay, extruded and baked; and polymer, which has a polymer resin base.

The whole range of leads are not needed by beginners and the number of line widths purchased will depend on the number of lead holders available. Users of lead holders and leads are likely initially to need about four line widths in the 6H to 6B hardness range. The softer the lead the larger the diameter/line width.

Pastels

Pastels are pigments ground with chalk, clay and other ingredients, bound with gum and manufactured in sticks. A large range of colours is available.

The Faber-Castell Polychromos range is made in 80 shades and Rowney's Artists' Soft Pastels in 193 colours including blacks and whites. This firm's square pastels in 48 colours are a useful introduction to the medium.

Pastels are fragile and softer than crayons, but this characteristic produces their distinctive effect. Pastel work must be fixed with a suitable fixative.

It is worth experimenting with all types of media, but it is unlikely that beginners will need more than a representative range of pastels. A good introduction to this medium is provided by Rowney in their introductory sets of 12 assorted, 24 half length and 12 square pastel sets.

Pencils

The most familiar drawing instrument is the black graphite pencil. The lead pencil is really made from a form of carbon called graphite. This is mixed with clay, extruded and baked in special kilns. The degree of hardness of the finished lead varies according to the proportions of clay used in this process. Figure 1.1 shows a pencil drawing.

The hardness of the lead is measured on a scale from 9B (very black and very soft) to 9H (very hard). HB (hard black) is approximately in the centre of the range. The softer the lead the more dense the tone it will produce. The effect of the lead also varies according to the type of drawing surface that is used. The smoother the surface the more even will appear the areas of tone.

Fig. 1.1   Pencil Drawing by Foundation Course student, Faculty of Art and Design, Barnet College

A pencil is a very subtle and sophisticated tool capable of a wide variety of effects and there is a very large choice of pencils on the market. There are coloured pencils in ranges of up to 60 colours and water-soluble, spirit-soluble, indelible and special-purpose pencils for a wide number of uses. Faber-Castell make useful life-drawing pencils in their Pitt range. These have a thick core and are made in three grades – soft, medium and hard. They also make a sanguine, sepia and white crayon version.

Many beginners like the pure graphite 12 mm hexagonal crayon pencils produced in grades HB, 3B, 6B and 9B. The black-lead Castell range has one of the largest gradings available from one manufacturer, from 8B to 9H.

Berol, another major pencil manufacturer make ten types of pencil ranging from their Venus Drawing, available in fourteen degrees of hardness from 6B to 6H, to their Alphex pencil, a large-diameter, hexagonal pencil with a dense, soft black lead very useful for large bold drawing. They also market a water-soluble blacklead pencil under the name Karisma Graphite Aquarelle.

The Mars-Lumograph range also offers nineteen degrees of hardness. Staedtler also makes the Tradition and Noris ranges with a more limited range of hardness.

Chinagraph pencils are specially made for marking polished surfaces including glass, acetate, china and film. The marks are impervious to water. The Royal Sovereign range has six colours and white.

Coloured pencils are made in large colour ranges. Polycromos pencils have a range of 60 colours and are soluble in white spirit. They include an excellent range of grey shades. Another very good range of colours is made by Rexel and called the Derwent. This firm has a choice of 72 colours in either pencil form or as 8 mm square blocks. Pencils and blocks can be purchased in sets and the pencils are colour tipped for easy identification.

The Karisma range from Berol is available in 72 different colours including several metallics and a choice of warm and cool greys. The Supracolor range of water-soluble colour pencils from Caran D'Ache contains 80 different colours.

Choosing a pencil from the range in a specialist retailers is really a matter of personal preference. Because pencils are cheap and easily obtainable they often get mislaid or borrowed, perhaps never to be found or returned. The tendency, therefore, is to buy more pencils than are really needed. The degree of hardness between grades is worth recording in a notebook. Make a 'grade' chart, small areas of tone representing all the grades, leaving gaps for the ones yet to be purchased. Never let pencils get too short so that control is lost over the marks they make. Get a pencil lengthener which will extend the pencil and its effective life. Always keep pencils sharp, literally razor sharp, by using only very sharp blades for sharpening.

A selection of about six pencils will be useful for general drawing. Try a 6B, 4B, 3B, 2B, H and a 2H.

Pens

It is important to be familiar with the different types of pens available for the artist and designer and to be aware of the tasks they are designed to perform. Buy a specialist pen if it is required for the work that is to be done. There are pens for calligraphy, lettering, technical drawing of all kinds, mapping, drawing on film, drafting, computing, plotting and many other categories.

Technical drawing pens

There are several types of precision technical drawing pens. These pens are sophisticated drawing instruments, expensive and requiring careful upkeep if they are to function efficiently. Some manufacturers make special ranges of pens for students. The main characteristics of technical drawing pens are the steel point used for drawing and the rechargeable, automatic ink feed which enables the pen to be constantly ready for use. The pen should not leak and the ink should flow easily and evenly.

Pens are sold either individually or, more usually, in sets comprising a number of pens capable of alternative line thickness. Some sets also include technical drawing instruments. The choice of line widths ranges from about 0.1 mm. to 2.0 mm. Interchangeable points allow for changes of line width, but if more than one line width is regularly used it makes sense to have more than one pen.

When coated drawing film is used the pen should be fitted with a tungsten carbide point as the normal stainless steel points are affected by this type of surface.

A technical drawing pen is something of a long-term investment. Design students have found the Marsmatic 700 trouble free and easy to handle. It is available in nine line widths, but it is unlikely that any beginner would need the complete set.

Ruling pens

These are one of the simplest forms of ink drawing pen. They are, however, sometimes difficult for the beginner to handle. Ruling-pen points are available for attaching to compasses.

Gillott's pens, with a wide range of nibs and different types of ink reservoirs are recommended for calligraphy, lettering and other graphic work. William Mitchell's pens are ideal for calligraphy.

1.3 DRAWING SYSTEMS

The visual world is normally seen through two eyes. This is called binocular vision. Because each eye sees a slightly different view of the world it is possible to judge distances and assess relationships in sizes. However, when information from both eyes has to be drawn on a flat surface, a picture plane, it is sometimes necessary to use a device called perspective if the final result is to give an illusion of the space that exists in reality.

Perspective

Perspective assumes one point of view, as if the world were seen with one eye closed. In order to draw 'in perspective' it may be necessary to first establish an eye level, an imaginary horizontal line across the picture plane representing the horizon. The higher the line, the greater the depth of the foreground, that is, the space in front of the 'horizon'. The angle at which any receding objects are viewed in relation to the eye level will change and the effect of this is to make identical objects appear to change in size as they recede, even over a very small distance. The apparent differences in size are exaggerated by the angles at which they are seen. The fixing of a 'horizon' can also determine whether receding diagonal lines slope upwards or downwards towards the point where they appear to meet, known as the vanishing point, which need not, however, be within the picture plane.

Horizontal lines that are parallel to the plane remain parallel, but spaced horizontal lines will appear to move closer together as they recede.

The spectator is always considered to be placed at a finite point in relation to the scene or objects and this point can be outside the picture plane.

Drawing systems are not always associated with the illusion of space. Egyptian artists of the period about 2600 BC used a stylised system of representing the visual world on the walls of their tombs. There is no attempt at perspective in these paintings. The relationships of size of the people, animals and objects are governed by their importance for the society for which they were painted. Similarly medieval paintings use a non-illusory system of drawing where symbolism has an important part to play. The needlework record of the Battle of Hastings in 1066, known as the 'Bayeux Tapestry', uses realistic imagery without perspective. In the twentieth century the Cubist paintings of Picasso and Braque also achieve an illusion of space without the use of formal perspective.

Plan

A horizontal section drawn, usually to scale, at a given level (see Fig. 1.2).

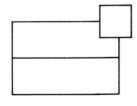

Fig. 1.2   Plan

Elevation

A vertical section, usually drawn to scale, at a given level (see Fig. 1.3).

17

Fig. 1.3 Elevation

Parallel projection

An alternative drawing system to perspective which, while dealing with spatial relationships in a systematic way, does not attempt to give the illusion of depth that is possible with perspective. With parallel projection the spectator is considered to be at infinity and the figures or objects are drawn without any change of scale in relation to their distance from the spectator (see Fig. 1.4). This system cannot, therefore, be used to create images that are intended to represent the illusion of space that can be achieved with perspective.

Orthographic projection

Parallel projections where the projected lines are perpendicular to the picture plane.

Axonometric projection

Orthographic projections in which the figures or objects are inclined in relation to the picture plane. There are three types – isometric, diametric and trimetric – of which the most commonly used are isometric projections, in which all three axes of a rectilinear object are shown at equal angles of 120° to each other, the dimensions along the axes being to the same scale (see Fig. 1.4).

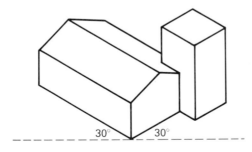

$30°$ $\quad$ $30°$

Fig. 1.4 Isometric and Parallel projection

Oblique projection

A parallel projection drawn with one aspect of the scene or object parallel to the picture plane and all other aspects inclined to the plane.

1.4 COLOUR

It is very difficult to be objective about colour, as everyone has a personal colour vision which is unique.

Colour depends on light. As light varies so colours can appear to change. What actually changes is our perception of the colour. The degree of emphasis placed on a range of tones is known as the tonal value and can help to define colours in a spatial context. Some colours appear visually to advance while others recede. A useful way of exploring tonal values is to work in monochrome, a range of tones from a single colour.

Colours are sometimes divided into warm or cold colours and can also take on an emotional context. 'Colour harmony' is a term used to describe a group of colours that appear to work well together. The best way to gain a knowledge of colour is to experience working from observation and recording the effects of colour.

Colours can be identified as either *primary* or *secondary*. Primary colours are red, yellow and blue. These three colours, together with black and white, are basic to all colour work. Secondary colours are made by mixing two primary colours together to produce a third colour:

> red mixed with yellow makes orange;
> yellow mixed with blue makes green;
> blue mixed with red makes violet.

Complementary colours

The primary colours (red, yellow and blue) each have a *complementary* colour. In theory the way to find the complementary colour of any primary colour is by mixing together the other two primary colours. The complementary colour of red, for example, is theoretically made by mixing yellow and blue together to make green. Green is the complementary colour of red. All this theory, however, is very basic but confusing. Having decided to find the complementary of a particular red, it is necessary to decide which tone of yellow is needed to mix with which tone of blue in order to make the complementary colour to the original red. It can become a tedious exercise. It is better to design a colour wheel using a set of primary colours with black and white and to make approximate complementary colours as shown in Fig. 1.5. This will involve making decisions about mixing colours. Another useful experiment is to observe the effects colours have on each other when placed in close proximity. The painter Johannus Itten has done some

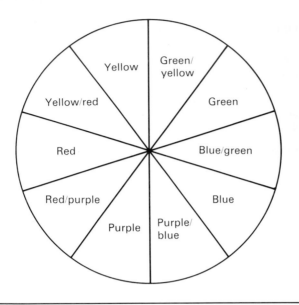

Fig. 1.5   Colour wheel

very interesting research on this (see bibliography (section 4.35) Birren, F. (ed) 1970).

The scientific study of colour and colour systems such as those of Chevreul, Ostwald and Munsell are of specialist interest for the beginner. The study of colour as a branch of physics should not be confused with the study of the appearance of colour.

Colour groups

Yellows:	Naples	Mars
	Lemon	Indian
	Cadmium	Yellow ochre
	Aureolin	Chrome
Reds:	Cadmium	Venetian
	Scarlet	Mars
	Alizarin	Indian
	Carmine	Rose madder
	Crimson Lake	Vermilion
Blues:	Prussian	Phthalocyanine (Phthalo)
	Indigo	Monestial
	Coeruleum	Cobalt
	Permanent	French ultramarine
Greens:	Cadmium	Phthalocyanine (Phthalo)
	Alizarin	Sap

	Monestial	Hooker s
	Terre verte	Chrome
	Oxide of chromium	Emerald
	Viridian	Cobalt
	Olive	

Whites:	Flake	Titanium
	Zinc	Chrome

Blacks:	Ivory	Mars
	Lamp	

Browns:	Raw sienna	Burnt sienna
	Raw umber	Burnt umber
	Vandyke brown	

1.5 PAINTING

The development of painting in the twentieth century has brought about radical changes which have also been affected by the availability of new materials.

Traditional oil painting, developed since the sixteenth century, has in many instances given way to work in a variety of different media or combinations of media (mixed media). One of the most significant changes has been the introduction of polymer emulsions. These have enabled painters to increase the scale and speed of their work and break with many of the traditional oil-painting techniques. The new paints can be sprayed, stained, dripped or thrown at the canvas. They can be applied with rollers or decorators' brushes. American painters in the 1940s and 1950s made basic discoveries with these new materials which continue to influence contemporary painting.

The economics of painting, particularly the high cost of making oil colours from the finest materials, has also increased the widespread substitution of polymer paints for oil colours.

1.6 PAINT/MEDIUMS/BRUSHES/VARNISHES

Acrylic	Aerosol
Alkyd	Egg tempera
Gouache	Metallic
Oil	Pigments
Polymer	Poster
Powder	Water-colour

Acrylic

Paint made using as a binder/medium a man-made resin derived from polymers or copolymers of acrylic acid.

Acrylic paint is fast drying with excellent adhesive qualities. It produces a clear, tough, flexible film that does not crack. The paint will dissolve in water when wet, is easily diluted and is waterproof when dry. By diluting one-to-one with equal parts of water and binder/medium it can be used as water-colour.

Mediums

Acrylic mediums act as a powerful gum as well as a binder. They enable the colour to adhere easily to a variety of surfaces and also help other materials to be incorporated into the paint. Mediums are available in a variety of forms. The most common are liquid, jelly and paste mediums. A gloss medium useful for making glazes of thin, smooth paint and a gel medium for thickening the paint are also available.

Surfaces

Highly absorbent surfaces such as hardboard should be primed with a suitable primer. Some good-quality emulsion paints can be used as primers but for durability a specially prepared acrylic primer is recommended as this will cover well, dry to a smooth white finish with the quality known as a 'tooth' finish and may be tinted. Rowney make an appropriate acrylic primer for this purpose.

A white primed surface will add to the luminosity of the paint. Acrylic paint should not be used on any surface that has been prepared for use with oil paint. Most manufacturers of canvases and boards make special ranges for use with acrylic paint. The cheapest method is to buy unprimed canvas, a suitable set of canvas stretchers and make up the canvas to individual requirements.

Acrylic varnish

To obtain a gloss finish use a water-based, flexible, transparent, lightfast varnish. This should be applied to the painting about twenty-four hours after it has dried. To stain, spray or apply a wash over a large area use a 'tension breaker' as the medium.

Additives; retarders

To slow down the drying of a painting use a retarder mixed with the colour.

Solvents

For removing areas of dried paint or cleaning colour from brushes or fabrics use an acrylic paint remover or solvent. Avoid using it in a confined space as the fumes could cause distress.

Brushes

No special brushes are required for acrylic paint. Nylon brushes are made for use with this paint but hog hair is quite suitable. Avoid letting the paint dry on the brushes: it is very difficult to remove. Always keep brushes in clean water when not in actual use and wash them thoroughly with soap and warm water when the work is finished. Use only stainless steel knives and a glass, china or plastic palette. Never use a wood palette. Acrylic paint can be used with a roller in the same way as domestic emulsion paint. Clean the roller and paint tray thoroughly after use.

Choice of colours

Winsor & Newton's introductory set of six colours is a good start for the beginner:

Burnt sienna	Crimson lake
French ultramarine	Mars black
Titanium white	Yellow ochre

Aerosol

For spray painting to give a waterproof, smooth, matt finish the Marabu Buntlack range of 28 quick-drying colours is ideal. These colours can be used on most surfaces and are made in two sizes, 300 ml and 600 ml. This firm also makes a smaller range of metallic paints in aerosol sprays.

Alkyd colours

A convenient substitute for oil paint, alkyd colours have the advantage of drying quickly. The paint remains workable for the length of a normal working day but will dry overnight. The colours can be reworked after drying by using a special solvent. Alkyd colours mix more easily than acrylic paint. They dry to a hard, elastic, waterproof film which does not crack. They can be thinned with white spirit, turpentine or a proprietary thinner. In this form they can also be applied as a glaze.

Mediums

No special medium is required for alkyd paint. Winsor & Newton's Liquin will increase the translucency and gloss of the paint. For thickening the colours use either Win-Gel or Oleopasto. All these mediums will also improve the drying time. Paste mediums should not be mixed with a brush. Traditional oil painting mediums can also be used but they will slow down the drying.

Surfaces

All surfaces suitable for oil painting can be used for alkyd paint. It is possible to mix alkyd and oil paint in the same painting, but always use the slow-drying oil colours on top of the faster-drying alkyd colours.

Varnishes
Use the varnishes available for oil paint. Retouching varnish can be used 24 hours after completion. Gloss- and matt-finish varnishes are available and should be added about one month after completion.

Solvents
Winsor & Newton's Winsol is a very strong solvent useful for removing dry alkyd paint. White spirit, petroleum distillate and turpentine will thin colours and will clean wet colour from brushes and palettes.

Brushes
Any brush suitable for use in oil painting can be used for alkyd paint. Always clean off brushes in solvent while working and thoroughly clean them in soap and warm water when finished.

Choice of colours
An introductory set of twelve colours is available. The minimum number of colours for effective working in alkyd is about seven. A beginner could start with tubes of the following colours:

Burnt sienna	Burnt umber
Lemon yellow	Cadmium red
Alizarin crimson	Phthalo blue
Flake white (large tube)	

Egg tempera

Eggs are traditionally used in the kitchen as a binder in cooking recipes and they have a similar binding effect when mixed with powdered pigment. Tempera is one of the oldest methods of easel painting and until the sixteenth century it was the most usual method. The use of egg yolks combined with powdered pigment and water enables the resulting 'tempered' mixture to dry quickly and produce a tough, permanent surface.

Tempera was traditionally used over a gesso ground. This is made from recipes using chalk combined with size and oils and produces a brilliant white painting surface. Egg Tempera is particularly suitable for the painting of miniatures.

Egg tempera can easily be made but must be used very fresh. It is also available ready prepared and makes an excellent underpainting for oil colours. Rowney's make a range of 25 colours plus three whites and also provide Gesso Powder and Rabbit Skin glue for preparing Gesso panels.

Gouache

Gouache is basically opaque water-colour paint. The paint gives a flat, matt finish and is ideal for design work. Gouache is water-soluble and the colours have varying degrees of permanence. They are available in tubes of various sizes. Manufacturers often describe this paint as designers' gouache. The colours can also be sprayed or used with a ruling pen. Gouache is normally intermixable with the whole range of water-soluble paints.

Winsor & Newton make a range of 124 colours and a similar range from Rowney lists 90 colours. Six basic colours, lemon yellow, cadmium red, cobalt blue, viridian green, lamp black and white, will make a useful introduction to this medium.

Metallic paint

One of the most useful ranges of metallic paint is that provided for the car industry. Retouching paint is available in a good range of colours and can be applied by aerosol to most surfaces. The aerosol can must be shaken thoroughly to mix the contents before use. Metallic markers are available from Edding in gold, silver and copper permanent, opaque ink. Rowney make a metallic finish rub-on paste in five finishes.

Oil colours

Oil painting is one of the longest established methods of producing easel pictures. The oil technique probably developed from the tempera methods which flourished up to the sixteenth century, but during the fifteenth century the established form of tempera painting began to be modified by the addition of transparent oil glazes over tempera underpainting. An intermediate stage then followed combining both tempera and oil techniques and this continued until the early seventeenth century.

One of the advantages of oil painting is the slow-drying properties of the oil which allow the painting to be developed layer upon layer with subtle effect. Originally, oil paintings were built up in a long series of carefully planned stages developing from full-scale drawings (sometimes called cartoons) through monochrome underpainting to the final work. Special techniques were developed to modify the later stages by the addition of layers of transparent paint called glazes. Sometimes paint areas were built up by a method known as *scumbling*, using opaque colours partially to overlay each other, giving an uneven effect to parts of the surface of the painting. These traditional methods are still in use and involve building up the painting in a series of layers, with each successive layer containing more medium, known as the fat-over-lean method. Each layer must dry thoroughly before the next is applied. The development of painting in the twentieth century has, however, encouraged the use of alternatives to the oil colour method (see sections on acrylic, alkyd and polymer colours).

It is not necessary for beginners to buy an expensive set of oil colours in a box, or special palettes, knives and easels, or the range of additives which are stocked by art shops. A basic set of colours from one of the inexpensive ranges such as Winsor & Newton's Winton range or Rowney's Georgian range might include the following colours:

Burnt sienna;	Burnt umber;
Lemon yellow;	Cadmium red;
Alizarin crimson;	Prussian blue;
Flake white (large tube)	

Add to this a bottle of good-quality linseed oil from a hardware shop, white spirit for thinning, a metal plate for use as a palette, some inexpensive hog-hair brushes, old rags and a suitably primed sheet of hardboard and this should complete a basic kit.

It is possible to make oil colours by mixing finely ground pigments with a good-quality linseed oil and petroleum distillate. There are also several types of medium on the market which can be added directly to ground pigment to make oil colours (see also section on pigments).

It is advisable to avoid purchasing tins of paint which dry out quickly once opened. Tubes of paint come in various sizes: the 22 ml to 38 ml size is practical for most purposes. Flake white should be purchased in the largest size available as it is likely that more of this colour will be used than any other. It is the fastest of the whites for drying and widely used in underpainting.

Mediums
Oil colours are soluble in turpentine or white spirit when wet. The usual medium is linseed oil, but poppy oil or safflower oil are also suitable. Another alternative is an alkyd medium, which has a shorter drying time than oil.

Surfaces
Canvas is the traditional surface for oil painting. It is manufactured both primed and unprimed. The cheapest is unprimed cotton. Other materials used are flax and jute. Canvas can be bought in widths up to 2.1 m (84 in) wide, but wider canvas can be purchased on special order.

Stretchers
Canvas must be stretched, ready for priming and painting, on special stretchers. It is possible to buy canvas ready-stretched, but it is much cheaper to purchase interchangeable stretcher pieces and buy canvas by the yard or metre. A variety of interlockable stretcher pieces will enable a number of canvas sizes to be made up. For stretching canvas a pair of special pliers is very useful.

Hardboard is recommended as an alternative to the more expensive stretched canvas. It is stable and can be reused if thoroughly rubbed down. A good-quality grade should be purchased and the painting carried out on the smooth side. The textured side produces a mechanical pattern in the surface of the hardboard which is difficult to eradicate. Large sheets of hardboard need strengthening at the back to prevent warping. All surfaces need careful priming to avoid the colour being absorbed into the surface. A good-quality emulsion paint is suitable. Several coats may be necessary to obtain a good luminous painting surface.

Brushes

It is worth investing in good-quality brushes. Always buy the best brushes that can be afforded. Cheap brushes soon lose their hairs and shape. For fine, detailed work sable brushes are ideal. They are very expensive, however, and blended hair brushes are a good alternative for the beginner. Hog hair is the traditional oil colour brush. Aluminium or seamless nickel-plated ferrules are preferable.

Always dry brushes thoroughly after cleaning and leave them upright when not in use.

Oil brushes are made in a range of 18 sizes from the smallest, 1, to the largest size, 18. There are 11 types of brush heads of which four types are most commonly used: Pointed (round); Square short (bright); square long; Filbert. A basic set of brushes should include at least one of each of these types. A No. 3 Pointed, No. 6 Square short, No. 8 Square long, a No. 10 Square long and a Filbert would be useful for the beginner.

Solvents

Solvents will dilute the oil colours. There are four main types:
1. Turpentine. This liquid will thicken if constantly exposed to light.
2. White spirit. Cheap – available in litre cans from DIY shops.
3. Petroleum distillate. This will slow the drying rate of oil colours when used as a medium.
4. Oil of lavender. Dries slowly.

It is cheaper to buy solvents from hardware or DIY shops, but the quality will not be as good as the types specially prepared for painters. It is also possible, but unnecessary, to buy ready-prepared mediums which are a mixture of oil and solvent.

Varnishes

Varnish has two main uses:
1. To restore the colour where a dull effect has been produced:
2. To give an all-over protective film to the finished painting.

Varnish tends to affect the character of the original colours although it will not darken oil colour. It is not usual to varnish a painting which has a heavy impasto effect unless it is necessary to use the varnish as a binder to hold the paint together. Varnish should always be used in moderation and preferably not at all. The main types of varnish are:

1. *Picture varnish*: Available in aerosols for coating the whole surface of a painting. It gives a slight gloss to the picture surface.
2. *Matt varnish*: Similar to picture varnish but giving a matt effect.
3. *Damar varnish*: Useful for restoring flat colours on an otherwise gloss or semi-gloss painting surface.

Pigments

A solid substance, organic or inorganic, which when finely ground is used to give colour to paint or varnish. Ground pigments are mixed with a binder to hold the pigment together. These binders are also sometimes known as mediums. The type of binder/medium depends on the type of paint to be produced.

Additives/varnishes/drying oils/mediums

Oils added to oil colours vary the drying rate of the colour. There are two types of oils commonly used in oil painting and they can be processed either naturally or chemically.

Linseed oils

Cold Pressed Linseed Oil. Produced naturally – expensive.

Sun-Bleached Linseed Oil. A pale, fast-drying naturally produced oil particularly useful for grinding in white pigment.

Sun-Thickened Linseed Oil (Fat Oil). A thicker version of the sun-bleached oil with a consistency useful for improving the flow of oil colours.

Refined Linseed Oil. Slows drying – chemically processed to increase gloss and transparency whilst reducing the consistency of oil colour.

Stand Linseed Oil. A chemically processed paler oil which gives a tough elastic film when dry. Slows drying but improves flow.

Drying Linseed Oil. Chemically processed to speed drying whilst reducing consistency.

Poppy oils

Sun-Bleached Poppy Oil. A naturally processed oil which is very pale

– useful for adding to whites and pale colours. Speeds drying whilst reducing the consistency of colours ground in Safflower oil.

Drying Poppy Oil. Chemically processed – reduces consistency whilst increasing the drying rate of whites and pale colours ground in Poppy or Safflower Oil.

Drying oils can be thinned with solvents such as white spirit or turpentine or the speed of drying can be increased by adding driers. Winsor & Newton manufacture a range of drying oils available in 75 ml bottles. Linseed Oil Cold Pressed, is also available in 500 ml bottles and Linseed Oil Refined can also be obtained in 250, 500 and 1000 ml bottles.

Manufacturers add to the bound pigment additives such as driers to increase the rate at which the paint dries, or retarders to slow the drying rate. All paint-makers have their own formulas for making paint and these are continually being improved. This sometimes means that paint from more than one manufacturing source is not intermixable.

Polymer paints.

There are two main types of polymer synthetic resin used in paint manufacture:
1. Polyvinyl acetate (PVA);
2. Acrylic (polymer or co-polymers).
Resins are combined with pigment and additives to produce paint which is available in tubes and other containers. Polymer paint can easily be made by adding a suitable polymer binder to powdered pigment. The only other medium required is water.

Suitable polymer binders are Rowney PVA Medium; Cryla Gloss; Matt and Glaze Mediums; Berol's Marvin PVA; and Winsor & Newton's Nacryl Acrylic Medium. Winsor & Newton list 65 dry-ground pigments available in 30 ml glass pots.

Polymer paints are fast drying and have resistance to yellowing. They will not crack and their excellent adhesive qualities enable them to be used on a variety of surfaces. The colours are intermixable within the individual manufacturer's colour ranges and they are removable with water whilst still wet. Easily diluted, these colours are highly water resistant when dry. The paint can be used as a glaze, for impasto work and for spraying. It can be applied in a variety of ways including by brush, knife and roller. Polymer paints dry quickly, so it is important to keep all implements in water when not in use. Cleaning should be in warm water with soap. A china, glass or plastic palette is ideal and can be cleaned with water if the paint is moist or scraped with a knife if it is dry. Soaking in water will help to remove stubborn dry colour. Always replace the tops of tubes and other containers immediately after use and ensure that the insides and rims of tops are clean. The medium acts as a strong adhesive and it is difficult to remove the tops from jars which have been left dirty.

Choice of colours

Rowney Cryla and Cryla Flow are available in 45 colours. Their System 3 Acrylic in 500 and 250 ml pots is available in 23 colours and in consistency is somewhere between Cryla and Cryla Flow, although the lesser strength of pigmentation is reflected in its more economic price. Winsor & Newton Acrylic colours are available in 50 colours and their Vinyl colour has a choice of 12 colours. This firm's vinyl colours are also available in 250 ml plastic buckets. A set of six 20 ml tubes of Artists' Acrylic is suitable for beginners.

Poster colour

Poster colour is a form of gouache which is opaque, water-soluble and ready for use from either tubes or the more familiar small glass pots. Poster colours are cheaper than designers' gouache. If funds are limited they are a useful alternative and they can be mixed with a number of other water-soluble paints. They are available in a large range of colours, but a set of six should be enough for a start: Lemon yellow; Otswald blue; Otswald red; Scarlet; Prussian blue or Black; White.

A metal or china plate as a palette and a jam jar is a useful water container.

Brushes

Soft brushes are essential. Do not use hog hair. Choose water-colour brushes from the most expensive range if possible. The price of brushes varies according to the type of hair used in the brush, from the very expensive sable to brushes made of a selection of mixed hairs from several sources.

A set of five brushes should be sufficient. Try numbers 0, 3, 5, 7 and 12. Aluminium or nickel-plated ferrules are best because they will not rust. Always repoint brushes when cleaned and store them upright.

Powder paint

The easiest form of paint mixing is powder colour and water. The result is a form of gouache or poster colour, very opaque and effective for bold design work. When mixed with a polymer medium such as one of the PVA mediums, the qualities of powder colour are greatly enhanced. The adhesive quality of the PVA enables the resulting paint to be used with effect on all types of surfaces. Large-scale, inexpensive, mural projects are therefore possible. The paint can be applied with rollers or ordinary household paint-brushes or the more refined water-colour brushes. Remember to wash out all brushes and other equipment thoroughly immediately after use. Powder paint is available in a limited range of colours.

Water-colour

Ground pigments mixed with water-soluble gums. This type of painting was developed in England in the late eighteenth and early nineteenth centuries. The water-soluble, translucent colours rely for their distinctive effect on the whiteness of the paper being overlaid with washes of transparent colour, with the thinnest colours being applied first. Pure water-colour painting is still a highly regarded craft, but many painters and illustrators now combine water-colour with other water-soluble media.

Water-colours are obtainable in the traditional box with replaceable pans or in tubes. The scale of water-colour painting is limited so the colours usually last for quite a long time. When purchasing tubes the smallest size may therefore be the best. The colours can be applied with brushes, sponges, soft cloths or fingers. If brushes are needed remember that water-colour painting can be done with any brush suitable for water-soluble paint. Find a personal method of working. There are lots of theories about how to paint in water-colours, but one of the greatest water-colour painters, J. M. W. Turner (1775–1851), experimented with these colours to great effect and did not conform to any rules.

The choice of paper is very important. It has to take heavy amounts of water and special care must be taken in choosing a good-quality paper. One way of effectively using a cheap paper is first to dampen it thoroughly with cold water, then fix it to the surface of a drawing-board by using gummed tape around the edges. Allow the paper to dry thoroughly before starting work and, on completion, cut the finished painting free from the board.

Some colours fade when constantly exposed to direct sunlight and care should be taken to protect finished work.

Water-colours are made in several grades. For beginners the cheapest grade is quite satisfactory. A set of six colours should be enough to allow for some experimentation: Lemon yellow; Vermilion; Crimson alizarin; Cobalt blue; Indigo; Viridian. Water-colour brushes are available in 16 sizes from the smallest size 000 to the largest size 14. Numbers 1, 3, 5, 7 and 10 will give a good range of brush marks. Take great care of brushes. Wash thoroughly after use, repoint carefully with the fingers and store with the brush hairs upwards. The price range of water-colour brushes is very wide and the larger sizes in the best-quality series are very expensive. Fortunately, manufacturers also make much cheaper brushes and, for beginners, the Cotman and Sceptre ranges from Winsor & Newton are good value.

1.7 BOARDS/PAPERS/SKETCH-BLOCKS/PADS

Boards

The word 'board' is used to describe a range of backings lined or surfaced with paper. Boards are made in a variety of thicknesses or weights (see p. 34). The papers are fixed to the surface of the board using special glues. Some boards have paper surfaces on both sides. The thicker the board the more stable will be the working surface. There are four main types of board which are in common use:

Bristol board

A pasteboard with a smooth surface ideal for making up packaging dummies. It is available in a range of thicknesses and a choice of sizes, from several suppliers including Daler-Rowney and Winsor & Newton. The surface, however, does not allow mistakes to be easily hidden unlike top-quality line boards which can be altered and re-used many times.

Line board

The most suitable surface for finished artwork. Good-quality boards will withstand erasure with a scalpel blade. The most famous line board is CS10 which is hand finished. Line boards will normally take work in line, wash and airbrush. These boards are expensive but a lower cost alternative is the Daler 'Truline' board.

Art board

There is a very wide range of boards available for finished work.

Illustration/fashion boards.   Frisk and Daler all have good ranges and for more specialist use Oram and Robinson have a Stripper board which is ideal for artwork/illustrations that have to be electronically scanned. Daler have a choice of 58 shades in their Studland and Ingres ranges. The Colourmount boards from Slater Harrison have a range of 79 shades in both four- and six-sheet thicknesses. This firm's Inglevale range has a choice of five sheet sizes from 508 × 635 mm (20 in. × 25 in.) up to 1524 × 1016 mm (60 in. × 40 in.) in a wide range of thicknesses. These boards have a smooth white, opaque surface on both sides.

Line and wash boards.   Hollingsworth Kent have two surface finishes NOT and Fine (HP) available from Daler.

Mounting boards for display and presentation.   Black, White and Coloured boards available from a number of manufacturers and suppliers. Daler's Studland mounting boards in A1 sizes and double-sided are obtainable in both black and white. Other manufacturers include Frisk, Oram and Robinson and Slater Harrison. Colour ranges vary from each supplier.

A black gel board available in 1400 micron from Slater Harrison is useful for the presentation of the work of designers, photographers and illustrators. A two-sided matt version is also available.

Televisual boards.   Slater Harrison's Mid-Blue board has a dense blue surface eliminating sheen under photographic conditions. Their TV caption Black Matt board has a dense black surface which makes it particularly useful for camera work.

Acid contamination

A neutral pH specification will prevent the artwork becoming contaminated with the acidity which is naturally present in wood-pulp products.

For the mounting of valuable water-colours or prints or any work requiring long-term protection the acid-free conservation quality boards from Daler are recommended.

Water-colour boards

Several suppliers offer excellent quality boards for work in water-colour including T. H. Saunders Waterford (Rag) mounted in three surfaces: Rough, NOT and HP. The Bockingford paper is also available mounted with the NOT surface.

Papers

Choosing the correct or most suitable paper is important if the best results are to be obtained. Papers in common use are:

Cartridge	Conservation/repairing
Cover	Crêpe
Drawing gummed	Fluorescent
Gummed	Handmade
Ingres	Kraft
Layout	Newsprint
Metal foil	Poster
Poster (MG)	Sugar
Print-making	Translucent/type/detail
Tissue	Tracing
Water-colour	

Handmade papers are now difficult to obtain. Japanese papers are obtainable from T. N. Lawrence & Son. They are usually unsized and therefore need careful handling. They are often made from fibres derived from the mulberry, used in Japan for the feeding of silkworms for the production of silk.

Paper quantities are usually measured in quires of 25 sheets or reams of 500 sheets.

Papers, and the boards on which they are supported, are sold in a variety of sizes, weights and quantities. Although standards of the

International Standards Organisation (ISO) are being applied to the paper industry, it is still possible to find other metric and imperial sizes quoted.

The main methods of determining the amount of paper to be purchased is by specifying the sheet size, weight and quantity. The density of the paper has an effect on the weight and this can be deceptive when comparing the weight of one paper against another. The thickness of boards is usually represented by reference to the micron (μ) thickness. $1\,\mu = \frac{1}{1000}$ of a mm therefore $1500\,\mu = 1.5\,\text{mm}$.

The weight of papers and boards is now almost universally given as grams per square metre (gsm or g/m^2). When imperial weights are used the references are to the weight per ream, i.e. 45 lb, 60 lb, or 140 lb.

Papers and boards are made with a variety of surfaces. The most common are:
(a) Hot Press (HP)   a smooth surface;
(b) NOT   a slightly rough surface;
(c) Rough.

In the following descriptions of papers, where a paper is also available mounted on a board, the letter (B) is shown after the name or type of paper.

Traditionally, papers used by artists and designers were made by hand from rags, but in nearly all cases this process has been replaced by machine or mould-made methods using a variety of materials including wood pulp and cotton. There are three basic types of materials used in paper manufacture: Ground wood (cheap), Sulphate pulp (ordinary) and Rag or Cotton (specialist).

Ground Wood: unpurified without additives. Used for Newsprint and Sugar Paper. Discolours very quickly.

Sulphate Pulp: the basis of most cartridge papers. The best quality are buffered with calcium carbonate to offset atmospheric acidity and will have some acidic elements removed. Such papers will not discolour nor adversely affect the colour applied to the surface.

Cotton: produced from a by-product of cotton mills. Also referred to as Rag paper from the time when this type of paper was made from the remnants of ships sails. The best of these papers are 100 per cent cotton and are machine 'mould-made', the mechanical equivalent of the earlier hand-making process. The result is a paper of regular and consistent quality and provides a rough or 'deckle' edge associated with hand-made papers. Also available are papers which mix cotton with a proportion of sulphate wood pulp or 100 per cent purified virgin pulp which excludes any recycled material. The cotton content determines the cost; the more cotton the higher the price. Examples of papers with such content are Daler's Bloxworth papers and Bockingford papers available from a number of suppliers.

Art paper
This is traditionally a china-clay coated paper which is mechanically passed through rollers to produce a hard, smooth surface. The term 'art paper' is used in a more general way and it is important to be specific if traditional art paper is required.

Card
A stiff paper useful for work where a flexible material is required. Card is very adaptable and can be rolled, twisted and easily cut. It is capable of taking thin washes of colour and can be used with a wide range of drawing media. Card has specific uses in fashion design, model-making, stage design and three-dimensional work of all kinds. It is also extensively used for display purposes.

Cartridge paper
This is the most common of all papers used for general drawing and is widely available in a variety of sheet and roll sizes and weights. The paper has a closely woven texture.

Cover paper
Originally produced to form the outside covers of books, this paper is now used for a wide range of purposes including work in chalk and pastel. The paper has a matt surface and can be obtained in a wide range of sheet sizes and weights. Daler have one of the largest colour ranges of 40 colours.

Crêpe paper
This paper has an elastic quality with a colour range which is ideal for display work. The colours are, however, quickly affected by exposure to sunlight and rapid fading can occur. Crêpe paper is not suitable for use with paint.

Drawing paper
This is the generic name given to a large range of papers including those sometimes classified as cartridge papers. Some papers in this group have the trade names of the makers such as Hollingworth Drawing Papers, which are ideal for architectural and engineering drawing and for designers' pencil roughs. Drawing papers are usually available with a choice of surfaces.

Fluorescent papers (B)
A range of very brightly coloured papers suitable for display purposes. Berol and Daler both have good colour ranges. The Day-Glo range from Slater Harrison includes plain, gummed, pulp and ticket boards in six colours.

Gummed papers
Available with either a smooth, shiny or matt surface with a gummed back in a wide range of colours. The paper is sold in squares, sheets or rolls and is ideal for decorative work.

Handmade papers
Traditional handmade papers are now difficult to obtain as only a few manufacturers still produce sufficient quantities for commercial production.

Ingres papers
These papers have a soft, textured, fibrous surface. A particularly good-quality paper is the Swedish Tumba containing 50 per cent rag. Daler have one of the largest colour ranges with 17 colours. The paper is particularly suitable for work in pastels and charcoal.

Kraft paper
A strong brown paper particularly useful for pen, ink and wash drawing. Available in sheets and rolls from several firms including Oram and Robinson.

Newsprint
An absorbent, unsized paper sometimes known as kitchen paper. Newsprint is similar to papers used for the production of newspapers. It is cheap but thin. Available in sheets and rolls and particularly useful for proof printing of all kinds.

Poster paper (MG)
An uncoated paper, machine-glazed (MG) and polished to give a high gloss on one side. These papers are primarily for use as posters and the sizes available correspond to the sizes of poster sites. Ideal for screen printing (see pp. 46–7).

Poster paper (B)
Papers designed for display purposes are also known as poster papers. The Inglevale range from Slater Harrison is available in 16 colours in both sheet and roll. This firm also has a seven-colour range of poster lined boards.

Specialist papers
CS2 (B).   A white paper ideal for illustration work using gouache, water-colours or dyes. Available as either HP or NOT surface in sheets and pads.

CS10.   An excellent paper for line work. This paper will take repeated erasings but will also give a clear image when used with a light box.

Particularly recommended for technical illustrations. Available in pads and sheets.

Hollingworth Kent paper (B)
This paper, which is available in HP and NOT surfaces, is recommended for work with designers' colours and gouache. It is also available as a line and wash board from Daler-Rowney.

Line papers (B)
In addition to the CS papers, a number of manufacturers make line papers. The Studioline range of lined boards from Slater Harrison includes a smooth-quality board suitable for finished artwork.

Sugar paper
A strong, absorbent paper with a toothed surface.* Available in a range of colours from Reeves and Berol. Suitable for work in powder colour, pastel, charcoal and crayon.

Tissue paper
Semi-transparent paper available in an excellent range of colours. The colours fade rapidly in strong sunlight and the paper will not take water or paint. Ideal for collage and all kinds of display work. Berol have a good range of colours.

Translucent papers
These tracing papers are made for specialist activities and have a high degree of transparency, together with an evenness of texture. It is important to protect the papers from variations in temperature or humidity which can affect the surface. Available in a variety of sizes and qualities. For general use the Winsor & Newton range is ideal. For specialist use the range of papers from Frisk, particularly their pads in A1, A2, A3 and A4 sizes (see Section 4.3) are excellent for design studio use.

Water-colour papers

T. H. Saunders (B).   A pure, rag-mould*, water-colour paper available with NOT, rough or HP surfaces and acid free to provide colour stability. Available from several firms including Daler-Rowney, Frisk and Winsor & Newton.

Bockingford.   A pure, wood-pulp, mould-made water-colour paper which takes washes particularly well. Acid free. This paper is less expensive than T. H. Saunders. Widely available from several firms including Frisk, Winsor & Newton, Daler-Rowney and Slater Harrison.

Refer to glossary.

Winsor & Newton's Watercolour paper

An internally and externally sized paper available in 30 × 22 in./762 mm × 559 mm sheets in three weights with a choice of three finishes: Hot Pressed, NOT/Cold Pressed and Rough. A heavier 260 lb/555 gsm is also available in NOT/Cold Pressed and Rough surfaces only. This paper can be obtained in sheet or block form. Acid free and made from 100 per cent cotton rag this range replaces papers no longer commercially available.

Water-colour pads

Papers suitable for use with water-colours are also made up into pads, usually of A2, A3, A4 and A5 sizes. The inexpensive Georgian Water-colour Paper, made up into pads in this way is available from Daler-Rowney.

Sketch-blocks

Sketch-blocks and pads are designed with a firm board base on which to work, with the top sheet having to be removed before work can commence on the following sheet. They are generally intended for use as either drawing or water-colour paper. Several manufacturers specialise in producing water-colour papers assembled in blocks and the papers available include Saunders Waterford and the Bloxworth range from Daler-Rowney.

Sketch-books

There are two main types of sketch-books. The more permanent type has sheets of good-quality paper carefully bound within stiff covers. The other type has detachable sheets, usually spiral bound. A sketch-book is an essential item for all artists and designers. It is one of the most useful ways of keeping together, in sequence, visual observations and notes. The famous sketch-books of Leonardo da Vinci are a supreme example of this kind of record. It is worth investing in a good-quality sketch-book with bound sheets rather than a spiral-bound book which is more difficult to maintain. Books containing excellent papers, including Saunders rough and NOT surfaces, are available and sometimes inexpensive books can be bought where a paper supplier or printer has bound together good-quality offcuts.

Suppliers of good-quality bound sketch-books include Daler-Rowney. Spiral-bound sketch-books are generally more easily available than the spine-bound type. The average paper weight is between 70 and 150 gsm and the range of sizes is from A1 to A5. Spiral pads are obtainable from several firms including Daler-Rowney, Reeves and Winsor & Newton.

Pads

Studio pads/layout pads

These are ideal pads for studio roughs and for the development of ideas in a visual form. Several firms produce high-quality paper pads, including Frisk who have a comprehensive range covering presentation, layout, marker, scrap, detail and tracing pads. All, except the marker and scrap pads, are available in four sheet sizes, A1 to A4.

The A plus pads from West Design Products (Schoellershammer) are highly recommended. The paper is made from dust bulk and is hand finished. The sheet size, although described using the ISO 'A' sizes, includes a border which allows for marginal sketches, trim lines, registration marks and notes. A similar range of tracing pads is also available. Other normal A-size pads can be obtained from Daler who make an 80-sheet pad in A2, A3 and A4 sheet sizes.

Tracing pads

Tracing pads are affected by changes in temperature and humidity which can cause cockling of the paper surface. Pads should be shrink-wrapped by the manufacturer. Frisk make two pads, one a lightweight pad (60/65 gsm) and one medium weight (90 gsm). Both pads are shrink-wrapped. Daler make 50-sheet pads in A2, A3 and A4 sizes, 90 gsm called the Designer Series, individually shrink-wrapped. For artists they make a 60 gsm paper pad called the Series A. The Hammer Micro-draft tracing paper from UNO (a division of West Design Products Ltd), is available in 63, 90 and 112 gsm pads, A0 to A4 sheets or in 762, 841 and 1016 mm-wide rolls.

1.8 PRINT-MAKING

The making of printed images on various surfaces is a well-established and traditional activity for both fine artists and print-makers. The making of a limited number of prints, known as an edition, is an effective way to control the production and price of prints. The development of photography has also given further encouragement to print-making and, for the popular market, the techniques of offset lithography and screen printing have enabled very large numbers of print reproductions to be cheaply and relatively quickly produced.

Limited editions

This term is used to refer to a small number of prints which are authorised by the artist and usually printed under the artist's control. They provide a guarantee to the purchaser that not more than a stated number of prints will be made and each print is signed and numbered by the artist.

Proof prints

Technically this is a print from the early, proofing stage of production. These prints are often hand-printed by the artist and, because of their rarity, are usually sold at a higher price than a limited edition. Proof prints are always individually signed and numbered by the artist.

Unlimited editions

With this type of print there is no control over the number of prints made and production can often run into thousands of copies. The artist's signature is mechanically reproduced and the prints are not numbered.

Reproductions. These are not prints but commercial copies, often varying in size from the original.

Original prints by artists such as Rembrandt and Goya are sometimes sold by auction in the major sale-rooms and can be purchased through fine-art* dealers. A number of galleries specialise in the sale of prints by contemporary artists. Outstanding collections of prints are held by the British Museum Print Room and the Victoria and Albert Museum Print Room, and most provincial and national galleries have important collections. There is a large collection of contemporary prints at the Tate Gallery.

There are three main classes of print-making: relief-printing; intaglio; planographic. Each of these methods is described below.

Relief-printing

Woodcuts

The ideal wood for woodcuts is soft with an even grain. The most commonly used is pear, but lime, cherry and sycamore can also be effective. The size of the 'block' is a matter of individual choice, but if it is intended to use it in conjunction with type its height must be the same as that of the type (2.33 cm). It is essential, too, that its sides be square so that it can be fitted alongside type in the printing 'frame'. Woodcuts should not be confused with wood engravings (described below). A woodcut print uses the flat surface of the wood with the grain running lengthways. It is useful to have a clear idea of the scale of the image to be made before cutting, but as the method of cutting is quite different from that of drawing it is sometimes best to let the image develop as the cutting proceeds rather than have too precise an idea of what to expect. Remember, the printed image on the paper will be the reverse of the image cut on the block.

If it is decided to draw direct onto the wood before cutting, then it is helpful to cover the cutting surface with a wash of process white such as that of Winsor & Newton, which is available in 30 ml pots. This will help to define the drawn image more clearly. Images can also be transferred to the block by using tracing paper which, when placed face down on the wood and redrawn from the back, will transfer the image to the block. It is also possible to cover the cutting area with a photographic emulsion, in controlled lighting conditions and thereby transfer images from film negatives.

Woodcutting tools
Any cutting tool will be effective on soft wood. The type of blade and the amount of pressure applied will influence the kind of mark and the subsequent effect on the print. Special woodcutting tools are available, such as gouges and scrives of various dimensions. All tools should be kept very sharp and not allowed to come into contact with anything other than soft wood. Suppliers of wood blocks include T. N. Lawrence, who also stock all the tools necessary for woodcutting.

Printing
Any paint or ink can be used for printing, and experimentation will produce a variety of images from the same block. If it is necessary to obtain an even cover of ink then specially prepared colours and a hand-printing roller should be used. The printing ink should be placed on a sheet of glass, evenly rolled and then lightly applied to the cut surface of the block. The block should then be firmly placed face down on the printing surface. Soft papers will take the image with the minimum amount of pressure. Heavier paper may require the use of a press. Blocks can be used for printing on a wide variety of surfaces including fabrics and plastics. Printing inks suitable for beginners are available from several firms including Daler-Rowney, Reeves and T. N. Lawrence. A woodcut by Dürer is shown in Fig. 1.6.

Linocuts
Lino is an inexpensive and effective method of relief-printing. It is available from Winsor & Newton in six sizes up to 400 × 300 mm. It is quite thick and has a plain, brown surface. Rowney stock lino in 1.5 × 900 mm rolls and T. N. Lawrence can supply lino mounted on wood to type height and lino by the roll.

The method of working is similar to that for woodcuts, but a major advantage in using lino is that the cuts can be made in any direction. Special line-cutting tools can be obtained such as Mitchell's lino cutters, which are made in a variety of shapes and are available in sets. T. N. Lawrence have a good range of lino-cutting tools.

Lino can be mounted on wood, chipboard or blockboard for printing and, if type high, can be printed alongside letterpress type. Large-scale linocuts are possible and all prints can be taken through several stages of development varying the printing, cutting and colours at each stage. The prints can be made using either oil or water-based inks. Oil-based printing inks are available from Reeves in 250 ml tubes in a range of eight colours. This firm also stock block-printing water-colours in 300 ml tubes in 16 colours. White spirit is needed to clean

Fig. 1.6   Woodcut – 'A Rhinoceros' by A. Dürer (dated 1515)

rollers and other utensils after printing with oil-based inks. A linocut by
Michael Rothenstein is shown in Fig. 1.7.

Wood engraving

This method of relief-printing enables subtle and sophisticated images to
be produced by cutting the close-textured end grain of boxwood. This
wood, however, is quite difficult to handle and great care should be
taken to prevent it from splitting. T. N. Lawrence stocks suitable end-
grain* blocks, type high and made to any size. Engraving can also be
done on plastic sheets and nickel-plated metal sheets. Such engravings
lack the delicate characteristics of wood engravings, but do provide a
more stable working surface. The technique of traditional wood
engraving favours the development of small, delicate images and a
master of this method of relief-printing was Thomas Bewick (1753–
1828). An example of Bewick's work is shown in Fig. 1.8.

Tools

There are two basic tools used for wood engraving. Line-making tools
and scaupers for clearing areas of wood. Either type of cutter is set in a
wooden handle, which is placed at an angle to the blade, to ensure that
the tool can be placed very close to the working surface to give
maximum control of the image. It is possible to obtain tools made to
individual requirements, but a set of standard tools is quite suitable for
the beginner. The line tools are called *gravers* and the tools for cutting

Fig. 1.7   Linocut – 'Cockerel Turning Round' (1956) by Michael Rothenstein

Fig. 1.8   Wood-engraving – 'Snipe' by Thomas Bewick from 'British Water Birds'
(1825)

curved lines are called *spitstickers*. A large *spitsticker* is called a *bullsticker*.
For hatching and producing even tones a tint tool is needed. Always
keep tools very sharp and only use them for engraving purposes. T. N.
Lawrence can supply a range of suitable tools.

Process

Wood engraving is carried out on a circular, leather pad filled with sand and known, appropriately, as a sandbag. Always work by turning the sandbag for changes in the direction of the cuts and never cut with the tool pointing towards the body.

Intaglio printing

Intaglio printing surfaces have the ink-carrying portions hollowed out; the whole surface is ink-covered then cleaned off, leaving the hollows filled with ink which is transferred when paper is pressed into contact. There are five intaglio printing methods in common use and these may be successfully combined to make mixed-media prints. All the methods use a metal plate as the vehicle for taking the image and transferring it to the paper. The traditional plate is copper, but zinc and steel plates are cheaper and, for etching in colour, steel plates should be used. The plates can be incised (etching, line engraving, drypoint), or the image developed by a combination of incised line and tone, or entirely tonal (mezzotint). The intaglio process is popular with fine artists and print-makers because of the individuality that can be sustained through the various methods, and the way that the image can be changed. Modern commercial printing methods now produce reproductions of intaglio prints which, however, lack the character of the originals.

Etching

Etching is the most popular of the intaglio methods. A coloured acid resist* ground is first spread over the plate. Then a special needle is used to draw through the ground and the marks made by the needle are subsequently bitten out by treatment in a nitric acid bath. The depth of the bite depends on the length of time the plate is left in the acid solution. Acid solution must always be made by adding the acid to water.

After treatment in the acid bath the plate is removed, cleaned and inked with a gauze pad or leather 'dolly'. Surplus ink is cleaned off with gauze and the flat side of the hand. The ink has now been forced into the areas burnt by the acid and the image originally drawn by the needle is then ready for printing.

The scale of etchings can vary from quite small areas about the size of postage stamps to large, poster-size prints. The process involves the use of dangerous acids and great care must be taken not to inhale the fumes and to wear protective gloves and clothing. Special exhibitions of etchings are occasionally mounted by such institutions as the British Museum, which has an outstanding collection, and the Victoria and Albert Museum.

An alternative method to the needle-drawn etching is photo-etching (see Fig. 1.9). With this method photographic images can be transferred to a photo-sensitised plate, prepared in controlled lighting conditions.

Materials for etching can be obtained from T. N. Lawrence who have a comprehensive range of tools, inks and other materials. Their French-style etching inks and French '88' ink range are particularly useful.

Fig. 1.9   Photo-etching – General Dynamics FUN 1965–70 'Transparent Creatures Hunting New Victims' by Eduardo Paolozzi

Line engraving

This is a direct drawing method on to a plate using a line tool called a Burin. It produces the most delicate drawn lines which are ideal for small-scale work. The plate is subsequently inked as for etching and printed on paper under pressure.

Drypoint

A similar method to line engraving. Drypoint uses a special steel point to scratch a line on to a plate. This method allows for freedom in the style of drawing and can be effectively combined with line engraving. The image has a short life, however, and few identical impressions can be taken. The inking process is the same as for etching.

Aquatint

This method enables tonal areas to be produced and can be combined with line techniques. Areas of tone are achieved by dusting the surface of the plate with granulated resin which is then melted over a low flame such as a Bunsen burner. This results in a grainy, porous surface through which nitric acid solution can bite, producing areas of tone to replace the areas dusted with the resin. These areas will, of course, be dark areas on the final print. To produce white areas it is necessary to stop out or isolate parts of the plate with a special varnish before dusting the surface with resin. An example of an aquatint is shown in Fig. 1.10.

Mezzotint

This process produces prints which are entirely tonal. The surface of the plate is abraded and tonal areas of great subtlety can be achieved by reducing, stage by stage, the depth of the abrasion. White areas are burnished and left smooth. This method can also be used in combination with other intaglio methods.

Printing papers

Unsized papers are ideal for intaglio as they are more absorbent and flexible. All the processes use dampened paper placed under pressure for printing.

Planographic printing

Planographic printing surfaces are level and prepared so that ink is accepted by some parts of the surface and not by the other parts. Ink-accepted parts of the surface may be greasy, the other parts being moist and ink-rejecting.

Screen printing

This is a method of printing images on a variety of surfaces, both two and three-dimensional, by forcing ink through a stencilled screen of fabric or metal mesh rather like forcing flour through a sieve. This

Fig. 1.10   Aquatint by a Foundation Course student of the Faculty of Art and Design, Barnet College

method is particularly suitable for printing flat areas of colour and is capable of using both drawn and photographic images. Two-dimensional screen printing on paper or fabric is the most commonly used system and is, therefore, the method dealt with in this section. The basic equipment needed is a wooden frame to carry the stretched screen; a suitable screen material such as organdie, silk, nylon or Terylene; a rubber squeegee for forcing the ink through the stretched screen and a drying rack to allow the printed surfaces to dry without touching one another.

The wooden frame.   The size of the frame determines the printing area but, as it is always possible to utilise a large frame for the simultaneous printing of more than one separate image, the smallest practical size needed is about 0.6×1 m (2×3 ft) inside-frame measurement. A separate frame is, ideally, needed for each colour to be printed, so work in four colours could require four frames. Frames can be handmade or purchased ready-made from a specialist supplier such as Sericol. In order to ensure that the colours are printed in exactly the same place on each print (correctly registered) the screen frame should be fixed to the base of the printing table and the corners of the sheets of paper marked on the table.

Screen fabrics   One of the best fabrics for making the screen is silk, hence the term silk-screen printing. The mesh of screen fabrics is graded from fine to coarse in a range of about fifty grades. Coarse grades have about 18 meshes to the square inch (size 0000) and the finest grades have about 200 meshes to the square inch (size 25). The coarser the mesh the heavier will be the deposit of ink on the printed surface. The fabric should be stretched on the frame using staples fired from a staple gun. It is important to obtain an evenly tensioned screen. Screen fabrics may need degreasing before use and suitable degreasers are available from Sericol.

Squeegee.   The rubber squeegee used for forcing the ink through the screen is mounted in a wooden handle. Blades are made in three grades: soft, medium and hard. For beginners the medium grade is ideal. The edge of the blade used for printing must be kept even and sharp.

Ink.   Screen-printing ink is available in four main types: Oil-based; Cellulose-based; Water-based; Plastic-based.
   Beginners are recommended to use oil-based inks which can normally be thinned and cleaned from screens with inexpensive white spirit. Cellulose and plastic inks require special thinners and solvents. All thinners and solvents are highly inflammable and give off strong fumes which should not be inhaled. Adequate ventilation is, therefore, essential.

Printing surfaces. It is possible to print on almost any surface. Beginners should experiment with as wide a range of surfaces as possible. For cheap, experimental proof printing, newsprint paper is ideal. Finished prints on lithographic paper are excellent and these papers are available in a wide range of finishes.

Image-making; negative image-making; paper cuts. The simplest way of making an image for screen printing is to prepare a paper stencil which can be cut or torn into the required design. These paper cuts are ideal for one-colour prints. For more sophisticated prints, use one of the special hand-cut stencil papers which, when cut, are ironed on to the screen, making an excellent bond between the stencil and the printing screen.

Painted stencils. A stencil can be painted or drawn directly onto the screen using a filler, a water-soluble cellulose. The filler should be used like paint. All the painted areas of the screen will, of course, resist the passage of the ink and the printed surface on the paper will comprise all the unpainted areas.

Negative/positive images; photographic stencils. It is possible to transfer a negative or positive image to screen by use of a photographic process. There are two methods both similar to the traditional way of making a photographic print. A negative image of an original can be made by transferring it on to a special transparent film, which is an emulsion-coated surface capable of deep tones of black. Same-size images can be transferred by direct contact and enlargements or reductions can be made by using a special process camera. The film must be subsequently developed using specified chemicals and then attached to the screen. Positive images can be made by actually coating the surface of the screen with a light-sensitive photographic emulsion, which is then allowed to dry. The coated screen must then be brought into firm contact with the negative image and exposed to a light source for a controlled period of time. In order to achieve complete contact between the original artwork and the prepared screen for both direct and film emulsion work, it may be necessary to place the artwork and the screen in a special vacuum exposure frame or sack which will enable all the air to be evacuated by means of an extractor valve and vacuum pump. Exposure to light hardens the emulsion on the screen that has received the image and the remainder of the emulsion can be washed away with warm water. After drying the screen is ready for printing. All manufacturers provide product information giving full details of these processes.

Printing. Ink is normally supplied in tins or tubes. Use a palette knife to transfer the ink to the taped inside edge of the screen. If the consistency of the ink is too thick to allow a smooth flow over the screen surface, then thin with an appropriate thinner.

Drying.   After printing remove the print and place it on a drying rack separate from other prints. Screen-printing inks vary in their drying times. Oil-based inks tend to dry quickly, but other inks may take some time to become thoroughly dry.

Screen washing.   After processing, and when the screen is required for a new image, all traces of inks and the original image must be removed with a suitable screen wash. The manufacturer's instructions should be carefully followed.

The simplest way of starting silk screen for the beginner is to buy a ready prepared screen and some additional fabric from a supplier. Reeves stock small printing frames ready fitted with an organdie fabric, baseboard, adjustable bar and squeegee. It is also possible to obtain a larger frame giving screen size of 353 × 305 mm. Organdie and polyester screen gauze is also available. Suppliers who stock Reeves's products can usually also obtain Profilm for making self-adhesive paper stencils, staple guns, staples for fixing the fabric to the screen, gummed paper strip, in rolls, for masking the edges of the frame and squeegees.

Sericol are major suppliers of screen inks and related materials and suppliers who stock Reeves's products can obtain Colorjet screen inks in a choice of ten colours, with black and white. Product information sheets are available giving full details of the properties and use of inks.

An example of a silk-screen print is given in Fig. 1.11.

Lithography

The lithographic print process is one of the most popular print-making methods and is capable of printing both direct and photographic images by reverse printing* or offset printing.* The process relies on the natural tendency of grease, contained in the drawing material, to repel water. Any greasy mark made on a lithographic plate is capable of being printed, but special drawing materials are normally used. There are two basic types of lithographic printing. The *direct method* produces a reverse image and the *offset method* produces a positive image. The direct method involves the transfer of an image to a zinc, aluminium or plastic plate by direct drawing on the plate, transferring a drawing from a transparency or photographic transfer. The offset method produces positive images by transferring the image from the plate to a special roller during the printing process which subsequently prints a positive image on the paper.

The plates
Lithographic plates are grained by the manufacturer to produce a surface which is capable of taking greasy substances such as inks, chalks

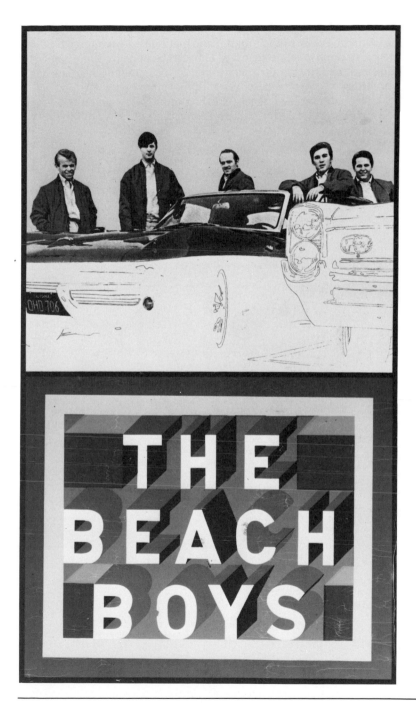

Fig. 1.11   Silk-screen print – 'The Beach Boys' (1964) by Peter Blake

and crayons which naturally resist water. This graining is not easily apparent to the eye or to the touch. Zinc plates must usually be treated before use to remove oxide coating. This can be done by using a special solution and then rinsing the plate in water. The grain of the plate can vary according to the type of work, with fine grain being used for plates which take photographic images. A lithographic plate can only be used for one image and one colour: an additional plate is required for every additional colour.

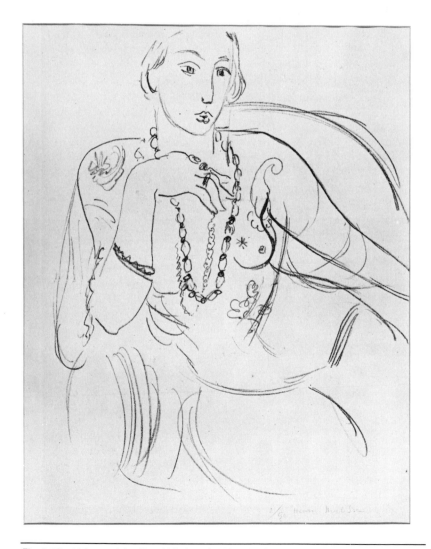

Fig. 1.12   Lithograph by Henri Matisse (1869–1954)

Image-making

The simplest way to make an image is to draw, with special ink, chalk or crayon, directly on to the surface of the plate. Litho ink is normally supplied in bars which need melting either in water, preferably distilled, or turpentine, until the required consistency is reached. Litho chalks and crayons are available in a range of hardness from soft 00 to hard No. 5. Alternatively, the image can first be drawn on a special transparent plastic film, which is capable of taking ink or pencil images, such as UNO matt drafting film. If more than one colour is to be used on the final print a separate image is required for each coloured area. Photo-opaque can also be used for drawing and correcting images or used as a completely opaque medium. Black crayons and waterproof drawing ink can also be used on transparent film. Colour work is simplified by using transparent sheets for all the drawing stages. A master drawing, in full colour, should be completed and overlays of transparent film used to isolate each colour area for the printing process. As each stage is complete, it is necessary to place corresponding registration marks on each sheet to ensure that all the overlays match on the final print. A more sophisticated method of colour separation can be obtained using photo-mechanical processes which ensure accurate registration, and these methods can be used with any printmaking method.

Inks

Lithographic inks are capable of being thinned to make excellent transparent colours and this enables a very wide range of tones to be achieved. Each colour to be printed requires a separate plate and, to ensure correct superimposition of the colours on the final print, it is usual to mark each plate with an identical registration mark (+) in each corner. However, the number of plates required is affected by the choice of colours and the sequence in which they are printed. For example, a blue printed over a yellow will produce a green. When planning the printing of colours it is essential to try and achieve the maximum use of colour with the minimum number of plates.

Photographic images

Line, half-tone* and continuous tone images can be reproduced on lithographic plates. Continuous tone images must first be processed using a dot screen to break up the image into a series of dots like the method used for producing newspaper photographs. The image is then transferred to a plate which has been treated with a light-sensitive photographic emulsion. Exposure to light hardens the drawn image and the remaining emulsion can then be washed off. Hunter Penrose Ltd are major suppliers of lithographic materials.

A lithograph by Matisse is shown in Fig. 1.12.

Specialisms in art and design

Graphic design

Audio-visual design
Advertising design
Book design
Communication design
Film/TV design
Graphic Communication
Illustration
Information design
Media design
Media production
Photography/film/video
Typographic design

Fashion/textile design

Carpet design
Clothing
Constructed textiles
Contour fashion design
Embroidery
Fashion design
Fashion illustration
Fashion merchandising
Fashion promotion
Fashion textile design
Footwear design
Industrial textile design
Textile design
Theatre costume design
Woven and printed textiles

Three-dimensional design

Automotive design
Ceramics

Computer-Aided Design (CAD)
Exhibition design
Furniture design
Glass
Industrial design (engineering)
Interior design
Jewellery
Metal
Plastics
Product design
Spatial design
Theatre design
Transport design
Silversmithing
Wood

It is possible to start a specialist course in one of the design areas from the age of sixteen by attending one of the full-time or part-time BTEC design courses. Many students, however, prefer to join a more general diagnostic course after leaving school and before deciding on their final choice of specialist study, and these students would expect to start specialisation at the age of eighteen. There are three major areas of design work and several minor areas. Full details are given in the reference section of the courses that are available. Each area has its own work methods and professional practices and, with the exception of fine art, its own career structure. Several of the areas overlap and it is often possible to work in two or more related areas. Some of the work such as Product Design requires a multi-disciplinary training, and other areas are very highly specialised such as medical photography or scientific illustration. Although fine art does not provide for a career, many fine artists find employment in related activities which demand the use of creative ideas.

In some design areas it is possible to work with relatively limited resources or as a free-lance designer with a small studio or workshop. These areas can include ceramics, jewellery, silversmithing, fashion design, textile design and graphic design, and the sections of this part of the book dealing with these subjects include some basic information on materials and methods to include the nature of the activities.

2.1 GRAPHIC DESIGN

The description 'graphic designer' is an all-embracing term for a person whose job is mainly the design of printed material, particularly for the advertising industry. Designers can, however, be specialists in one or more areas, including typography, packaging, all types of illustration, television and film graphics, book design, layout, stamp design, logos*, liveries, house styles* and audio-visual presentations. The graphic designer is involved with the creative, economically viable presentation of words and images so that they achieve their maximum effect.

Normally a designer works to a brief set by a client which may outline the nature of the task, the financial limitations, the market for which the product is aimed and possibly the concept that the designer has to project. Sometimes a designer is responsible for the total house style of a company or institution or the promotion of a product such as a perfume or a brand of petrol, but often a team is given the task under the supervision of an art director who will bring together other specialists such as copywriters and photographers. Designers must be aware of ethical, social and legal restraints and be familiar with typography and printing methods and photography. Draughtsmanship and drawing skills are essential. Above all the designer must have creative ability and the professional expertise to translate ideas into visual images.

The design process

Before starting the detailed work on a design, the designer must obtain as much information as possible about the needs of the client. The most appropriate method of reproduction must be chosen and the size of the finished design established. In some cases, such as the column width of a newspaper or the size of a railcard for an underground train this will be predetermined. If colour can be used, the designer must decide how it is to be used. Sometimes a particular type of paper might need to be chosen and this could be influenced by cost and the choice of printing process. The actual words to be used, known as the copy, their emphasis in the design and the choice of appropriate type styles and sizes must be decided and a decision on the possible use of photographs or illustrations might be made. Once decisions have been reached on such basic points, the designer is ready to proceed to the layout.

Employment for designers tends to be either in a studio, which is usually a fairly small, independent specialist firm possibly servicing several larger firms, or in an agency which can be a large international company dealing with a number of major clients. The influence of the work of the graphic designer can be seen everywhere from postage stamps to Guinness posters. Much of the work has a short life and the industry therefore tends to consume large numbers of creative ideas over relatively short periods of time.

Layout: scamps/roughs

Initial ideas, possibly noted in pencil on scraps of paper are known as *scamps*. Such ideas, often from several sources, are brought together by the designer who is to plan the layout. This involves producing a number of alternative designs called *roughs*, usually on layout paper using feltmarkers. The roughs enable the designer to experiment with various ways of dividing the space required for text and pictorial areas and establish any margins or grids that may be required. Eventually the final version of the layout will be produced, often in consultation with the client, and this is known as a *finished rough*. It will indicate the final positions of all the components of the design.

Grids: modular design

Pre-printed grid sheets are now normally provided for any publication which follows a standard format for more than one issue, such as magazines, and also for book production. The example shown of a grid sheet in Fig. 2.1 is the Longman standard text grid sheet showing the layout of this page, and Fig. 2.2 is another example from this book of how authors set out their ideas for the book designer. The designer can vary the amount of text or the size of the illustrations in relation to the grid. The grid can show the column widths of text and also margins and can be given either horizontal or vertical emphasis.

Dry transfer lettering

These are hand-lettering methods using transferable type prepared on plastic-backed sheets or transfer cards. The characters are transferred by hand pressure using a blunt tool or special spatula. A large range of symbols is also available. Graphic designers find useful the co-ordinated lines and dots, points, graduated tints, borders and rules which are available on transfer sheets. Self-adhesive coloured films and papers are other design aids and, for sign-writing or similar work, PVC transfer lettering can be used on surfaces such as glass, metal, plaster and painted wood.

Typography

All graphic designers need to have a thorough knowledge of typography and it is possible to specialise in this subject. Designers are responsible for the selection of a suitable typeface for a particular job and this depends on a number of things, including the nature of the work, the designer's style, the client's requirements and the printing methods. There are hundreds of typefaces available and new ones are being designed each year. Besides being available in roman and italic, each typeface usually includes a number of variations of style and size. Type variations can be in condensed or extended forms and are often available in different weights such as light face, medium face, or bold face. The small decorative strokes usually shown at the top or bottom of a letter are called serifs, and 'sans serif' simply means 'without serif'. Recognition of typefaces, for example Univers or Helvetica, is made visually, and can only be achieved after long practice. However, there are recognition aids available for the beginner, in the form of printed

The actual words to be used, known as the copy, their emphasis
in the design and the choice of appropriate type styles and sizes
must be decided and a decision on the possible use of photographs
or illustrations might be made. Once decisions have been reached
on such basic points the designer is ready to proceed to the layout.

Employment for designers tends to be either in a studio, which is
usually a fairly small, independent specialist firm possibly servicing several larger firms or in an agency which can be a large
international company dealing with a number of major clients. The
influence of the work of the graphic designer can be seen everywhere
from postage stamps to Guinness posters. Much of the work has a
short life and the industry therefore tends to consume large numbers
of creative ideas over relatively short periods of time.

Layout: Scamps/Roughs. Initial ideas, possibly noted in pencil on
scraps of paper are known as Scamps. Such ideas, often from several
sources, are brought together by the designer who is to plan the layout. This involves producing a number of alternative designs called Roughs, usually on layout paper using felt markers. The Roughs
enable the designer to experiment with various ways of dividing the
space required for text and pictorial areas and establish any margins or grids that may be required. Eventually the final version
of the layout will be produced, often in consultation with the client,
and this is known as a Finished Rough. It will indicate the final
positions of all the components of the design. Grids. Modular
Design. Pre-printed grid sheets are now normally provided for any
publication which follows a standard format for more than one issue
such as magazines and also for book production.

Insert figure 2.1

The example shown of a grid sheet in Figure 2.1 is the Longman stan-

Fig. 2.1   Longman standard text grid sheet with prepared text

58

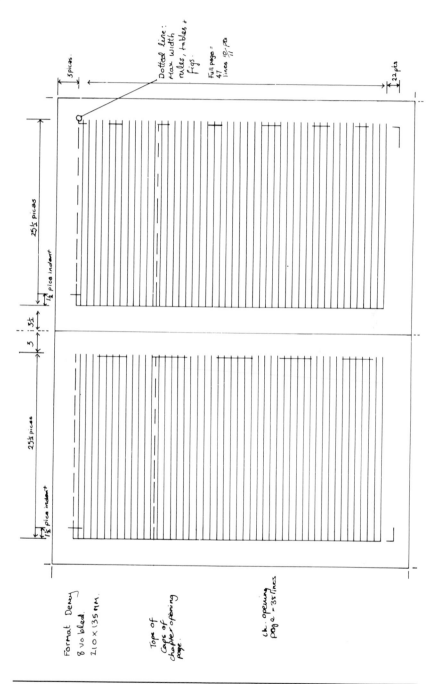

Fig. 2.2   Page layout for this handbook.

sheets of various typefaces and sizes available from the Monotype Corporation or other suppliers. Typefaces are also referred to by series numbers, for example 'Times Roman 327'. In typesetting specifications it is usual to specify both the name of the typeface and the series number.

Composition methods – printing

Photo-composition

Photo-typesetting is a more economical method for type composition. The process is keyboard activated and produces text ready set as a photo-negative or as a positive print from which can be developed the printing plate. Photo-typesetting machines use a computer or micro-processor to translate the input from the keyboard, select the correct typeface and print size and store the copy. The operator, who can also be the designer, can see the composition of the text develop on a visual display unit (VDU) as the copy is typed into the machine and corrections can be made during this stage. The introduction of these compact machines into design studios enables designers to work directly with the actual copy that eventually forms the printed page. Photo-composition is also used for the production of 'display' type. The storage of information is by either magnetic tape of floppy disk.* The machines have large storage capacities and one disk can store hundreds of thousands of characters. Text that has been processed by a photo-typesetting machine is described as *filmset*.

Micro-processors

The development of technology using micro-processors enables the graphic designer and the typographic designer to produce images in either black and white or colour by use of a digitising pad, an electronic pencil and an appropriate software* program. The results can be instantly seen on a VDU and, if required, they can be printed and incorporated into layouts. Organisations such as the BBC are using electronic character generators to produce a wide range of graphic images.

Copyfitting

When large areas of text have to be specified, the designer has to ensure that the available space will accommodate the required number of characters. This process is called 'copyfitting'. Type scales, which resemble rulers, are useful in measuring the width of a typesetting and, for small areas of type, a character count is a reasonably accurate measure of indication as to whether the print size chosen is likely to fit the space available on the page. The designer is helped by working from a typed script which is usually set in either an élite typeface, with twelve characters to the inch, or in a pica face, with ten characters to the inch.

If, however, there is a lot of copy to be fitted, then a standard copyfitting table can be used to decide the number of characters for the space available in the layout.

Experimentation with type is essential for the beginner, and hand-lettering is a useful method of becoming familiar with letter forms. The spacing between characters is important. Serif characters, for example, do not all occupy the same amount of space on the printed page. A study of typefaces is a useful introduction to typography.

Illustration

There are two main types of illustration work: *technical illustration*, which is a highly specialised method of technical drawing, and *general illustration*, which includes book, magazine, film and television illustration. Illustrators are generally self-employed and work as freelance illustrators or as author/illustrators on, for example, children's books. Technical illustrators are concerned with the illustration of technical processes and machinery and sometimes specialise in aeronautical, electrical or mechanical engineering illustration. Most illustrators use similar tools for producing their work, but general illustrators are sometimes involved in print processes which are craft-based, such as wood engraving or etching. An airbrush is a useful tool combining compressed air and colour to produce a fine, controllable spray through a special, pen-shaped tool.

Illustrators need to be familiar with typography and the whole range of image-producing processes. Photography is a very valuable resource and film can be used as a method of visually recording information required for illustration or combining photographic techniques with traditional illustrative work. Some illustrators specialise in animation work using a film camera which is combined with a special camera mount with both a movable carriage and a baseboard.

Technical illustrators need high standards of numeracy as much of their work requires very accurate detailed drawing to scale.

Artwork

The final stage in the presentation of a design is the preparation of all the materials required for printing, possibly including text, photographs, line drawings, illustrations and colour separations. This is called the *artwork*. This is sometimes done by the designer and sometimes by other specialists. The artwork can be assembled to the designer's instructions in a positive form ready to be photographed or as a photo-negative on film ready to be transferred to the printing plate. If the artwork is to be produced with positive material the text may have already been typeset and will be positioned in the final layout as appropriate. The process of assembling artwork is known as *paste up* and specialist paste-up artists are employed to carry out this work in some firms.

Television

Graphic designers who work in television are responsible for the design and supervised execution of title sequences, credits and all programme material of a graphic nature. The recruitment is generally from applicants who have successfully completed a BA or equivalent level course in an appropriate subject. Graphic design assistants must also have had previous successful training to BA or equivalent level and some experience in advertising or related industries is an advantage. Design assistants work, under supervision, with graphic designers and holiday relief vacancies sometimes occur at the BBC. A most important requirement is good draughtsmanship.

Graphic assistants

The staff who work in the Graphic Design Print Room at the BBC are known as graphic assistants. They produce a wide variety of typographic material for film and television productions. The work includes credit captions and small graphic properties of all kinds, and the production methods include advanced electronic character generators. Experience in letter assembly and typing is desirable. Accuracy in the presentation of work is essential and an art school training is an advantage.

2.2 PHOTOGRAPHY/FILM/TELEVISION

Photography

Work in this area has close links with a number of other professions including journalism, advertising and fashion. There is also the area of scientific and technical photography. All art and design students should own and use a camera, preferably one with interchangeable lenses. Ideal are 35 mm reflex cameras which enable the actual image to be viewed through the lens, and excellent cameras are available from reputable second-hand camera dealers. It is always worthwhile purchasing a camera case for the protection of the camera and, for expensive cameras, it may be advisable to insure them against loss.

The relationship between the photographer and the artist and designer can be a working partnership or the roles can be combined where the artist/designer/photographer is one person, undertaking all aspects of the work.

Creative photography

This category includes artist/photographers who use the medium to promote their philosophical and social ideas in visual terms and includes some aspects of experimental photography. Sometimes artists, such as R. B. Kitaj, Andy Warhol and Robert Rauschenberg, have used photography as part of their creative work and some American painters, such as Don Eddy, Richard Estes and Richard McLean, have used photographs as the source material for their paintings. Creative photography also includes the work of photographers who explore aspects of the visual world in photographic terms, such as Richard Avedon, Bill Brandt and Snowdon. This group belongs to one of the oldest traditions of the medium, going back to the early pioneers, such as Margaret Cameron.

Specialist photography
The most famous of this group are the fashion photographers, such as David Bailey, but this area also includes the specialists who work in laboratories and hospitals or with the police.

Photo-journalists
This is possibly the largest group of professional photographers, who either work as employees for national and regional newspapers or as free-lance photographers for newspapers and magazines.

There is some overlap between all these areas, and a photographer may work in two or more areas. However, the personal reputation of a professional photographer is often built on the quality of image-making relating to a small area of specialisation.

Materials
The range of chemicals and papers available for processing film material is very extensive. A number of manufacturers including Kodak provide publications giving detailed information about their products.

Chemicals.   Kodak make a range of chemicals suitable for beginners with limited resources who wish to experiment with developing their own images from film negatives. Their D–76 Developer Powder is available in quantities suitable to make one litre of liquid developer and their Dektol developer is made in both powder and liquid form. The Kodak Indicator Stop Bath arrests the development of the image immediately and is economical. When exhausted the stop bath liquid turns purple. Available in one-litre containers. A useful rapid-hardening fixer is Kodak Unifix suitable for both films and papers – fast working and economical. It is available in 500 ml sizes.

Papers.   Contrast grades, Kodak papers:
1.   Soft. This grade is suitable for high-contrast negatives.
2.   Normal. Particularly suitable for negatives of medium contrast.
3.   Hard. This grade is suitable for low-contrast negatives.
4.   Extra Hard. A grade for negatives of very low contrast.

A good, economically priced general-purpose paper for printing negatives by the dish-processing method is Kodak Kodabrome Print RC (resin-coated) Paper. It is available in contrast grades 1, 2, 3 and 4 and is of medium weight.

Papers are normally available in a range of alternative surfaces. 'E' – Lustre Luxe, 'F' – Glossy, 'N' – Semi-matt are the most common. The base thicknesses of papers vary. Single, medium and double weight indicate the range of weights easily available. The speeds of papers also vary and are based on the ANSI (American National Standards Institute) scales. Papers are usually identified by terms such as Slow, Medium, Fast or Very Fast to identify speed of development.

Colour processing

It is possible to carry out colour processing with fairly limited facilities, but automatic commercial printing methods are very competitive in price and may make the purchase of the necessary equipment and chemicals uneconomic. For experimental work, however, it is very useful to have a simple colour-printing system available.

Colour prints can also be produced using special films and cameras such as those manufactured by Polaroid and Kodak. The size of the original print is limited, but commercially produced enlargements are possible. No additional chemicals are required to produce the original image. The special film contains the necessary processing chemicals and the manufacturer's instructions should be closely followed.

Lighting

It is often necessary to provide special lighting for photographic work and specialist publications give full details of the wide range of equipment available and its suitability for different types of work. A simple flash unit, preferably attached to the camera, may be necessary if photographs are to be taken in poor lighting conditions such as museums. Flash cubes enable a number of exposures to be made using one cube. Electronic flash units are capable of a large number of exposures under controlled lighting conditions and these units can be battery/mains operated.

Experimental photography

Experiments are most important for beginners whose previous experience of photography may have been limited. A good starting-point is a simple photogram made by placing thin, two-dimensional objects in the film holder on the enlarger or using larger, three-dimensional objects placed directly on the enlarger baseboard. Combinations of these two methods are also possible and effective. No film negative is required. The enlarger lamp acts as the light source and, when the objects are placed directly in contact with the printing paper, the enlarger lens is not used. The results resemble silhouettes of the objects and effects of great subtlety can be achieved. The enlarger is used to create photographic images without the use of a camera.

Film sizes

Colour film is normally available in 110, 120, 126, 127, 135 and 620 sizes with either 8, 12, 20, 24, or 36 exposures per film. Black and white film is normally available in 120 and 135 sizes with either 8, 12, 20, or 36 exposures per film

Sheet film

The traditional sheet film sizes, quarter-plate, half-plate and whole-plate, are being replaced with the International range of 'A' sizes.

Film speed

The speed at which film is receptive to light is measured in DIN (Deutsche Industrie Norm), ASA (American Standards Association) and ISO (International Standards Organisation), all of whom provide calculations on which it is possible correctly to judge the exposure time required for films. The ASA/DIN/ISO number may need to be used both in connection with the camera setting and the setting of an exposure meter. The higher the number, the faster the film.

Colour film

Storage.   Colour film requires careful storage for optimum use and manufacturers recommend refrigerated storage for all professional quality film. Amateur film is specially made to 'mature' in storage and can be kept at room temperature (21 °C).

Colour print film.   Kodacolor VR 100 (ISO 100) and VR 200 (ISO 200) both provide excellent results at a budget price. Store below 21 °C. VR 100 available in 120 size; VR 200 available in 110 and 120 sizes. Kodacolor Gold 200 Film is available in a wide range of sizes from 135 to 620. Store below 21 °C.

Colour slide film (35 mm).   Kodachrome 25 Film (daylight) is ideal for all bright light conditions. Store below 21 °C.
Kodachrome 25 Professional Film (daylight) specially made for fashion, product and fine-art situations. Store at or below 13 °C.
Kodak Ektachrome 50 Professional Film (tungsten) is for product, art-work, advertising and other subjects requiring artificial tungsten lighting conditions. Store at or below 13 °C.

Black and white print film

35 mm.   Kodak Panatomic-X Film useful where big enlargements are required. Store below 21 °C.

120.   Kodak Panatomic-X Professional Film, slow-speed, high-definition film. Store at or below 13 °C.

135. Kodak Plus-X Pan Film. A good all-round film for use in most lighting conditions. Store below 21 °C. Also available in 35 mm size.

Filters

A wide range of filters for general use on camera and enlarging lenses are made by Kodak under the trade name Wratten Filters. Each filter is designed for a particular use and many are capable of absorbing colours and ultraviolet radiation. Other filters include those which enable light intensity to be reduced by a definite ratio and filters for lowering or raising the effective colour temperature of a light source.

Film and television training

The National Film School in Buckinghamshire provides full-time courses for students who wish to study for a professional career in film and/or television. The main criterion for entry is creative ability and there are no formal academic entry requirements. Entry is, effectively, by open competition and some students enter having recently completed university courses or courses at a similar level in an art and design college. The school, therefore, operates at the level of a postgraduate institution.

Four areas of activity are defined by the school, from which the student programme is drawn:

1. Technical or conceptual training in a workshop, either singly or as part of a group.
2. Screenings, discussion, lectures or seminars not related to specific production activities.
3. Personal or group production, including writing, or as a member of a crew on such a production.
4. Attachment to a professional production company.

The Royal College of Art provides two-year postgraduate (MA) courses in Design for Film, Film Direction and Film Production.

Some courses combine the study of photography with film and television, such as the London College of Printing Visual Communications course and the West Surrey College of Art and Design Photography, Film Video and Animation course.

2.3 FASHION DESIGN

The professional designing and construction of fashion garments, shoes, millinery and accessories is a very specialised activity. Students who wish to study for one of these areas normally first complete a BTEC National Diploma (diagnostic) Course or a Foundation Course in Art and Design to confirm their choice of specialism or a BTEC National

Diploma or Certificate Course in a relevant specialised area. These courses can then be followed by Degree or BTEC Higher National Diploma courses and postgraduate courses are also available. Mature students may be eligible for these courses or may join part-time City and Guilds courses, usually attending a college for one day per week.

Forecasting

A fashion designer can only work with the colour ranges and cloths that are available. Their availability depends, to a certain extent, on accurate forecasting of fashion trends. A number of organisations and individual designers carry out forecasting to help cloth manufacturers plan their production. In Europe one of the main forecasting systems is that carried out by organisations closely associated with the production and promotion of specific cloths such as the International Institute for Cotton and the International Wool Secretariat. Meetings of such organisations take place about eighteen months before the garments are required in the shops and result in forecasts of colour and design trends being passed to cloth manufacturers. Forecasting relies on a sensitive response to possible influences and can include social trends, the effects of changes in popular culture, films, television and major international exhibitions. Without efficient planning it would be impossible for manufacturers to cater for the international mass market, as they need time to plan their production, which can involve manufacturing millions of metres of cloth for a major change in fashion styles. The major forecasting organisations have forecasting rooms containing samples of the proposed new cloths and colour schemes and where trade representatives can see the ideas proposed for forthcoming seasons.

The design process

The designer usually starts the planning of a new range of garments by choosing fabrics and colour schemes for possible translation into clothes. The choice of materials is sometimes influenced by a personal forecast of fashion trends. The particular concept for a new style is seldom based on the personal needs of the designer. Such concepts are more likely to be affected by the availability of cloths and the possible demands of the particular age, social and economic groups of the people who are to buy and wear the clothes. Having chosen a range of fabrics and colours, the designer sketches possible alternative variations of styles, ensuring that the finished sketches are capable, if necessary, of being translated, by mass-production techniques of manufacture, into identical copies of the original design in a range of sizes. To enable designers to work systematically, the actual designing can either be carried out on blocks, which are permanent records on card of standard body sizes, or by making up a garment from a cheap fabric directly on to a dress stand of the appropriate size. Designs which are made up in this way are called *toiles*. In both cases the design has finally to be translated into a paper pattern and a skilled technician called a grader is required later to adjust the pattern according to the sizes required for the production garments. A standard block for women's clothes normally consists of five pieces:

1. Front bodice;
2. Back bodice;
3. Sleeve;
4. Front skirt;
5. Back skirt

The designer adjusts the block or the toile to suit the new style, and the paper pattern, which is then cut, reflects the nature and style of the new garment, including additions such as collars or extra seams. Both blocks and stands can change their proportions and shape according to the prevalent fashion style. An Edwardian block, for example, is quite different from a 1980s block, and similarly with the shape of stands. The majority of commercial patterns are planned on blocks, and are therefore cut flat. After the cutting of the fabric, which is another skilled craft, undertaken by trained pattern cutters, the pieces of cloth are made up into a sample garment by a skilled machinist. Large manufacturers often have a sample room which is set aside for the production of 'one-off' garments so that they can be approved before being mass-produced in the clothing factory. Computer programs are now available which will undertake the cutting of fabric, and the development of micro-processors is also having an influence on production methods.

Theatre costume design

Although the work of a theatre costume designer is similar in many ways to that of the fashion designer, the nature of work for opera-houses, television and film studios and theatres requires a special interest and ability to design original or historical costumes, often using materials and methods which are a simulation of the real thing. Career opportunities are limited. Some designers who work in this area qualified as fashion designers and subsequently specialised, while others have completed a professional course of training in theatre costume design. Like stage designers, costume designers have to work as part of a team, usually under the direction of a theatre director. In some cases a production director will co-ordinate the design of the lighting, staging and costumes for a production, particularly if the resources are extensive, such as for an opera. In such cases the influence of the costume designer could be minimal and limited to interpretations of the creative ideas of other people. Costume designers who work in large theatrical, opera or ballet companies will often have the resources of workshops and specialist staff. The attributes of the fashion designer, combined with an innovative flair for improvisation, are a good background for this kind of work.

Fashion illustration

This is a specialised area of illustration and is usually done by trained fashion designers who have the necessary creative drawing ability. Most fashion design courses include illustration as part of the programme of study. Employment opportunities are limited to free-lance work and there are close associations with fashion journalism. A fashion illustration is shown in Fig. 2.3.

Footwear design

The design of boots and shoes for men, women and children is another specialised design activity and training can start from the age of sixteen years on BTEC courses. There are, however, very few centres as career opportunities are limited. Some fashion courses include the design of footwear in their syllabuses and specialist courses are provided by the Cordwainers' Technical College in London, which provides vocational courses up to production management level. Leicester Polytechnic provides a CNAA degree course in footwear at both BA and MA levels.

2.4   TEXTILE DESIGN

Textile designers usually specialise in either printed, knitted or woven fabrics. With printed fabrics the design is imposed on the material by one of several alternative printing processes, of which screen (flat bed or gravure), heat transfer (Sublastic – trade name for transfer paper printing process using heat) or spray are the most common, depending on the type of fabric. Knitted and woven fabrics incorporate the design as part of the manufacturing process. A number of designer/crafts people combine the roles of designer and manufacturer by specialising in the printing or painting of individual fabrics by hand or in hand-knitting or hand-loom weaving. Constructed textiles combine two or more processes. Industrial manufacturing in the United Kingdom has been adversely affected by foreign competition particularly from the Far East and, for some fashion areas, from Italy. Much design work, however, is still carried out by British designers who may work as free-lance designers for several manufacturers or market their designs through agents in the USA, Europe or Japan. Designers also work as staff designers for individual firms, possibly producing a 'house style', while others work for design groups or studios for joint marketing and exhibition purposes.

Fabrics vary according to their use which can include menswear, women's wear, furnishing (domestic and contract) and specialist, which can include such items as fabrics for aircraft, train and car seats. The largest design areas are possibly for fashion and household textiles. The

Fig. 2.3   Fashion illustration by BTEC National Diploma in Fashion Design student, Barnet College

nature of the fashion industry, with its emphasis on changing styles and seasonal collections, can involve the designer with a large turnover of designs from year to year, but the furnishing industry is traditionally conservative, although some areas such as household linens, curtain fabrics and co-ordinated schemes can involve a designer in responding to fashion trends. There are three basic textile printing methods suitable for beginners:
1. Relief printing;
2. Screen printing;
3. Resist printing.

Relief printing

Block printing is a relief-printing process similar to the woodcut printing methods used by print-makers. The design is first traced and then transferred to the surface of the wood block by placing the tracing face down and burnishing it from the back. The areas of the block to be printed in colour are then painted in a water-soluble paint and cutting tools used to remove all the unpainted areas of wood. Fabric printing blocks are generally cut deeper than woodcut blocks as fabric is less resilient than paper to pressure. Although this method is ideal for simple, one-colour designs, multicoloured prints can best be printed using a wood block with a felt inlay to absorb and evenly distribute the colour to the fabric. A separate block is required for each colour. Metal strips can also be used to make intricate patterns. The strips are hammered into the softwood block to produce a thin, metal edge which becomes the printing surface. Registration marks for multicoloured work are essential and are made by inserting brass pins, known as pitch pins, in the corners of the block.

A firm, stable printing table is required. The table should be covered with a thick woollen blanket which must be completely encased in a waterproof sheet such as Neoprene. Over this should be stretched a smooth, plain cotton fabric backing cloth which stops the ink from marking the waterproof cover. The fabric to be printed should be pinned to the cloth at intervals, depending on the type of fabric, to prevent movement.

Screen printing

The basic techniques for textile screen printing are similar to those for print-making on paper. Metal frames are generally used because they are lighter than wood and more easily handled and they do not warp when wetted for cleaning. The fabric is fixed to the screen with adhesive lacquer covering the face side of the frame. The warp and weft of the fabric is placed parallel to the sides of the frame. Screen-printing tables need to be longer than those required for block printing as the area of the screen is considerably larger than a normal wood block. The table should be prepared in the same way, however, with the addition of a suitable registration rail and stops placed exactly parallel to the outside edge of the print table. This will enable the screen to be fixed accurately to the printing surface and the registration angle bar on the screen will enable it to be keyed into the appropriate stop point. The stop points are placed at the distance apart of the exact 'drop' of the repeat. The whole width of the cloth is printed at one time using one screen for each colour. The length of fabric to be printed is subdivided and allowed to dry, followed by numbers two, four and six, etc. which prevents 'marking off' on the underside of the screen. Squeegee blades need to be hard and the edges are usually V-shaped.

Colour separations, if required, are usually prepared by hand, using Kodatrace and photographic opaque. Photo-mechanical separations are sometimes necessary when particularly difficult photographic imagery is being used or if a detailed trichromatic separation* is required. The mesh size of the screen is important. The number of threads to the square centimetre chosen for a particular screen depends on the nature of the artwork. Textile meshes can usually be slightly coarser than those required for graphic prints because the image is often of a larger size.

Resist printing

Batik is a method of resist fabric printing which originated in Java (Indonesia). It is based on the ability of wax to resist cold water and uses brushes and a traditional tool called a *tjanting* to draw designs in liquid wax directly on to a fabric from which all artificial dressing has been removed. The fabric can be waxed and dyed several times in more than one colour and, when completed, the wax can be removed by boiling the fabric in water.

Tie-dyeing is another resist method which utilises tied knots, sewn threads and the incorporation of small stones and pebbles held into the fabric by elastic bands or threads to resist cold-water dyes. The fabric can be dyed in several colours or in several tones of the same colour, removing, after each dyeing, a section of the tied, sewn or knotted design. It is also possible to add new elements to the design at any stage. Batik and tie-dyeing methods can be combined in the design of the same fabric, and the traditional colour for tie-dyed fabric is indigo.

Repeating patterns

The production of repeats in design work for fashion fabrics is not usually required and the drawing based on the original idea, known as a *croquis*, after the French word meaning an outline, is usually sold not in repeat. A designer will normally charge an additional fee if a repeat is required. Designs for furnishing fabrics, however, are normally sold in repeat. The number of designs in a collection often determines the amount of time spent on repeat work. When fashion and furnishing fabrics are similar, both in imagery and style, repeat work can be a positive disadvantage. There are a number of types of repeats of which the most common are block, brick, interlocking, half-drop (mirror vertical, mirror horizontal and mirror diagonal), turn about, foulard and various spot repeats. Examples of repeat patterns are shown in Fig. 2.4.

Textile printing colours and dyestuffs

Dyes require different methods of application for different types of fabrics and also have special characteristics. Some dyes completely permeate cloth while others do not permeate at all or only partly permeate. Paints, inks and crayons are available for working directly on to fabrics. The imagery conceived for a print often dictates the print method to be used and also the type of fabric.

Suppliers

T. N. Lawrence can supply wood blocks and the necessary cutting tools and inks.

Weaving

There are three basic weaves used for the production of cloth:
1. *Plain weave*: Producing a fabric which is lightweight, reversible, firmly constructed and durable.
2. *Twill weave*: A variation of plain weave using more warp than weft when the cloth is to be warp faced and more weft yarns when a weft face is required. A diagonal weave is produced across the cloth.
3. *Satin weave*: This uses long warp yarns which pass over a number of weft yarns before passing under a weft yarn. Generally, this weave produces a lustre to the surface, but it has poorer durability than plain or twill weave.

There are two main types of yarn used for weaving in wool: woollen yarn and worsted yarn. Woollen yarn, when made up into woven cloth, has a bulky, fuzzy texture and is produced from yarns in which the individual fibres come together in a random way. Worsted yarn produces woven cloth which has a smooth texture and is more durable than woollen cloth. This yarn is composed of long fibres of wool which are parallel.

Cotton, silk, flax and man-made fibres are also extensively used, either individually or in mixtures, as yarns for weaving.

Knitted fabrics

Machine knitting

The machine process for manufacturing knitwear is similar to plain or stocking stitch knitting by hand. The yarn is machine-knitted into a series of horizontal rows or loops called *courses* and, as the process

Block Repeat

Brick Repeat

Half- drop

Mirror Vertical half-drop

Mirror Horizontal

Interlocking

Fig. 2.4   Repeating patterns by BTEC General Art and Design Diploma course student, Barnet College

continues, vertical rows of loops are formed known as *wales*. The term 'fully fashioned knitwear' refers to a process where the shape of the garment is determined by the machine increasing or decreasing the number of stitches and forming the shape of the finished garment. When the required shape is cut from a knitted length of fabric the process is known as 'cut and sew' knitwear. Changes in the structure of knitwear fabrics are achieved by using different-sized needles. Some knitted fabrics have an elastic quality and the appearance of horizontal or vertical ribbed lines.

The most common form of knitting machine is a flat bed which carries the yarn backwards and forwards along a row of needles. These machines can be either power- or hand-operated. Some machines can provide for the introduction of unspun fibres, thus allowing the making of fabrics with a soft, deep pile, and these machines also incorporate a carding unit which can produce parallel fibres for incorporation into the yarn. Warp knitting machines knit together yarns from the warp and this method is used to produce very open-weave fabrics.

Trent Polytechnic, Nottingham, offers a BA (Hons.) three-year course in Knitwear Design.

Hand knitting

Woollen, worsted, cotton, man-made and blended yarns are available for hand knitting. The majority of yarns are composed of two or more yarns twisted together and known as *multiple-ply yarns*. The greater the number of yarns the thicker the ply. Effective hand knitting relies on the correct tension being maintained and this is affected by the size of needles used. If the tension is too loose, smaller needles are required and, where the tension is too tight, larger needles are needed.

Surface pattern design

This is an area of design related to textiles, but normally dealing with pattern designing on materials and products other than textiles. This includes designing for wallcoverings, giftwraps, decorated consumer products (such as tins, trays and mugs), ceramics, laminates, tiles, paper cups, plates, napkins and other products which incorporate surface patterns. Co-ordinated designs, where one pattern is used on a wide range of products, maximise the potential point-of-sale outlets and markets. The largest area of co-ordinated design is probably household textiles where one pattern can be repeated on curtains, bed linen, upholstery, table linen, cushion covers, lampshades and floor rugs.

The range of materials can vary from chintz cottons to PVC fabrics and from ceramic tiles for the bathroom to plastic mugs for the kitchen. There are specialist courses in surface pattern design and several textile design courses include this area of work in their syllabuses.

2.5   THREE-DIMENSIONAL DESIGN

This area of work encompasses the largest group of design activities, ranging from the self-employed designer/craftsman to the industrially based designer working as a member of a team for a mass-production industry. One unifying factor is the necessity for all those concerned with these activities to have a developed awareness, creativity and ability for dealing with design problems involving space, volume, form and decoration. Many aspects of three-dimensional design also require the ability to make accurate mathematical calculations and to work to fine degrees of measurement. Numeracy is, therefore, most important. All areas require skill in handling tools and a knowledge of the characteristics of a wide range of materials.

A number of courses are available which offer a broad general introduction to certain specific areas of work and then provide an opportunity to specialise in one or more chief study. Other courses concentrate on specific design areas such as ceramics, while some offer a programme of study which is an amalgam, for example wood/metal/ceramics/plastics.

Ceramics

Ceramics is one of the oldest recorded crafts in the world and evidence of the work of potters has been found dating from thousands of years ago.

The majority of contemporary potters are self-employed or work as free-lance ceramic designers. The ceramics industry employs technicians and craftspeople as well as designers, but modern industrial methods of production offer relatively little opportunity for a career as a ceramic designer in full-time industrial employment. The relative simplicity of pottery methods, however, enables the beginner to learn the basic craft skills quickly and, if this craft ability is linked to creative design potential, then it is possible to develop a professional practice as a craft potter producing tableware and decorative pottery of all kinds. Some ceramic designers' work is non-utilitarian, producing 'fine-art' objects using a variety of methods and techniques.

Clay

The basic material for all pottery is clay, which is found in most parts of the world and chiefly consists of two main types, china clays, pure white and rather difficult for the beginner to use, and ball clays, which are available in Britain as either red (terracotta) or white clays, easy to use because of their ability to be easily shaped and moulded by hand. Ball clay is normally supplied either as prepared clay or as powdered clay which requires the addition of water to make it workable. The preparation of powdered clay is difficult for beginners with a limited amount of space and resources. It is possible to use local clays, particularly those dug from sites near river banks. Used clay can easily be reclaimed and reused, providing it has not been previously heated in a kiln, a process known as firing. All clays require firing in a kiln to make the clay objects durable.

Prepared clays are easily available for two types of hand-made pottery:

1. *Earthenware*: The most popular form of pottery for beginners. The clay objects have to be fired in a kiln to about 1100 °C, and this process gives them a smooth, slightly porous surface.
2. *Stoneware*: This pottery needs firing to a higher temperature than earthenware, needing between 1200 and 1350 °C. The resulting surface is non-porous and the objects will be stronger, but with limited possibilities for decoration.

The first firing of pottery in a kiln is known as a *biscuit* firing.

Tiles
It is sometimes difficult for beginners to make tiles which have an even thickness and regular shape. Variations caused by the qualities of the clay and the effects of drying and firing often cause warping and distortion to handmade tiles.

Moulds
Moulded dishes of all shapes and sizes can be simply made. Always try to design an original form on which to make the mould. There are two main types of mould: press moulds, where the dish shape is obtained by pressing the clay into a plaster of Paris mould, and hump moulds, where the dish shape is obtained by forming the clay over a moulded plaster form. Other pottery forms can be made by wrapping clay around a preformed shape of wood or similar material which has first been covered by newspaper to stop the clay adhering to the shape. Cylinder construction is particularly easy by this method.

Experiments
Always experiment with hand-making methods in order to explore the potential of clay as a means of creative expression. The plastic qualities of clay allow for a wide variety of treatment. Avoid stereotypes and repetitive designs copied from commercial ceramics. Use the basic construction methods to explore modelling possibilities. Visit the ceramic collections at the British Museum, the Victoria and Albert Museum, the Percival David Foundation in London and the provincial collections in centres such as Stoke-on-Trent, Cambridge, Oxford and Durham. Contemporary pottery of a high standard can often be seen at craft centres and at some art galleries.

Thrown pottery
The making of pottery forms by means of a revolving wheel is another traditional method of construction. Foot-operated (kick) wheels and electrically-operated wheels enable the potter to make a hollow pottery

form by fashioning the clay as it revolves. Throwing pottery forms is usually easier for beginners on kick wheels, where greater control can be obtained. The process depends on accurate centring of the clay on the wheel before the thrown form can be developed. The ability to throw pots varies and some students find it impossible to achieve. It is only a part of pottery-making and, as plenty of other methods exist, the beginner should not be discouraged if unable successfully to use the wheel.

Decoration
Clay, in its plastic form before drying, can be decorated in a number of ways including pinching, fluting, indenting, incising and scratching. Such decoration then becomes part of the structure of the object.

Slip casting. Pottery forms can also be decorated, before firing and when the clay is leather hard, by using a mixture of clay and water called 'slip'. It can be poured into dishes to form a decorative covering or used on pots by dipping them into a bucket of slip. It can also be used in a slip trailer, a nozzle fitted with a rubber, slip-filled bulb, which, when pressed, makes delicate patterns of slip on the clay.

Glazes
After the first (biscuit) firing in the kiln, pottery can be coated with a glaze made from silica and then fired in the kiln for a second time. This method will produce either a transparent or opaque glazed surface, depending on the nature of the materials. Ready-made glazes in powdered form are easily obtainable. A glaze is a mixture of silica and a flux, specially prepared for pottery, and, with experience, it is preferable to experiment and make individual glazes.

Kilns
It is not necessary to fire pottery only in an electric, gas or oil-fired kiln. Raku pottery, named after a form of Japanese pottery, uses an outdoor, hand-built kiln which can produce porous earthenware at a temperature of about 700 °C, fired by wood or a solid fuel such as coke. Small electric kilns are capable of glaze as well as biscuit firings, but may not be capable of reaching the temperatures required for stoneware. Oil- and gas-fired kilns are generally used only by the professional potter and are capable of the full range of process firings necessary for commercial production.

Kiln furniture
Fireproof kiln furniture for supporting the pottery in the kiln, such as shelves, known as bats, stilts and props, is specially made and the interior kiln temperatures can be indicated by pyromatic cones, known as Seger cones, which bend when specified temperatures are reached. The cones are placed in the kiln after the pottery has been packed and in

a position where they can be observed, during the firing, through a peephole. More sophisticated kilns usually have a pyrometer attached to the outside of the kiln, linked with an interior kiln device which gives an accurate reading of the kiln temperature.

Damp cupboard

If it is necessary to retard the drying-out process of clay, for example if more work is required than can be achieved in one working session, then the clay object should be wrapped in polythene and kept in a moist atmosphere. A special damp cupboard may be necessary if a number of objects need to be kept in this state.

Pug mill

When large quantities of clay are needed a pug mill is used to 'mince' the clay and obtain a mixture of an even consistency. Such clay may not need wedging but will require kneading before use.

Tools

Very few special tools are needed. A basic list should include a kitchen rolling-pin and wooden spoon together with the following specialist items: rubber kidneys, for shaping; boxwood modelling tools; slip trailers; wire loop modelling tools; a wire cutter, turning tools. Special pottery tools can be obtained from several firms including Clayglaze and Wengers.

Display design

Display designers are employed by all the major departmental and chain stores to design and make the window and interior displays which promote the sale of goods. Different seasons of the year, such as Christmas and Easter, need special displays and other promotions may require lavish transformations of the interior of large stores. The nature of this work often requires much of the actual fitting of new displays to take place when the stores are closed for normal trading. Some firms employ designers who are permanently based in the stores, while others employ travelling designers who move from town to town changing displays. Display designers require creative abilities in both two- and three-dimensional design, lettering and typography and a knowledge of printing processes. A developed sense of colour and texture, together with drawing skills, are important. There are a number of BTEC courses available in this area of design.

Film and television design

Many of the skills required by film and television companies are those which are equally applicable to other design areas such as graphic design, interior design, stage design and theatre costume design. There are some specialist courses which specialise in training for film and television design.

Basically the television design team usually consists of a designer and a design assistant. The usual route for entry to posts in the BBC is by appointment as a design assistant. Promotion to designer is normally by internal appointment. Design assistants should have training in architectural or exhibition draughtsmanship and must normally have successfully completed a suitable advanced course in an art and design college. The BBC does not run any training courses. Holiday relief design assistants are sometimes appointed from students who have successfully completed a BA or equivalent level course in such areas as interior design, theatre design or architecture, but can also include those who have trained as painters, sculptors, print-makers and industrial and furniture designers.

Furniture design

There are basically two types of furniture designer. There are those who both design and make individual items of furniture and usually work for themselves or in small companies, and those who only design for the mass-production market. Sometimes, however, there is some overlap between these two categories. The designer who makes individual pieces of furniture has to have very high standards of creativity and craftsmanship as the marketing of the product relies on the personal reputation of the designer and on the uniqueness and appropriateness of the finished item. Mass-production designers are often designing for a specific market and work as either free-lance designers for several firms or as an employee of a major manufacturing company. Aesthetics, ergonomics* and a knowledge of the characteristics and capabilities of a wide range of materials, together with high standards of numeracy and draughtsmanship, are necessary. The traditional furniture industry is usually conservative in its attitude to design, and new ideas are often slow to appear in the mass market. The most important developments have been in the use of new materials and new production techniques using advanced technology. Some designers specialise in the conservation and restoration of antique furniture, working for specialist dealers, museums or national institutions.

Glass design

Courses that specialise in glass design sometimes combine the study with ceramics. Edinburgh College of Art offers a specialised glass course. The Royal College of Art provides postgraduate courses, combined with ceramics, leading to the award of M.Des.(RCA).

Interior design

Interior designers tend to work as free-lance designers for private clients or in design partnerships under contract to large public companies, such as restaurant and hotel chains and breweries, where they are responsible for the total look of the interior of buildings. Exhibition design is often part of the job of the interior designer. It is sometimes difficult to establish a successful career as it is nearly always necessary to work with architects who often wish to be responsible for the interior of buildings they have designed. However, the largest architectural practices often employ interior designers as part of their design teams, and the ability to work with other specialists such as structural, heating, ventilating and electrical engineers, together with architects and graphic designers, is most important, A highly developed sense of period and style, colour and texture, together with numeracy, draughtsmanship and drawing skills, are all necessary for the professional interior designer.

An interior designer can be required to specify all the requirements for an interior, ranging from small items such as door handles and light switches to carpets, curtains, furniture, wall and ceiling surfaces, kitchens, bathrooms and toilet equipment and the choice of cutlery, china and glass.

Industrial design (engineering)

Industrial designers work in the electronics, plastics, engineering and allied industries, in the automotive and aerospace industries or in design practices serving these industries. The work has close associations with engineering design, ergonomics, aesthetics and design history, and workshop studies form a part of the professional education and training. The range of manufactured items designed by industrial designers is very wide and includes land, air and water transport of all kinds and consumer products, including all the major household items such as refrigerators, cookers, television sets, vacuum cleaners, hi-fi systems, radios and videotape recorders. Also included are the specialised machine tools and other apparatus used for the manufacture of these and other items. A science/design-based general education to GCE 'A' level standard is the normal minimum entry requirement with possible emphasis on mathematics and physics. The Central School of Art and Design, London, offers a three-year First Degree Course leading to the award of BA Honours, and similar courses are available at Leicester Polytechnic, Leeds Polytechnic, Manchester Polytechnic, Napier College, Sheffield City Polytechnic and Teesside Polytechnic. Coventry (Lanchester) Polytechnic offers the only First Degree Industrial Design Transportation Course in the United Kingdom. The Royal College of Art offers postgraduate courses in industrial design.

Jewellery and silversmithing design

One of the most distinctive features of this area of design is that many designers make up their designs themselves rather than have the work done by craftsmen. Their response to materials is therefore a very practical one and a thorough knowledge of the processes is essential for the professional designer.

Jewellers must have an inherent ability to work on a small, three-dimensional scale with particular reference to the decoration of the human form.

There are basically two types of jeweller:

1. The designer/maker, who works in precious metals such as gold, silver and platinum and also in precious stones. Much of this work is traditional in design and is usually purchased either as an investment or as an outward show of wealth. Traditionally, the jewellery trade is divided into 'mount-makers', who design and construct the whole piece but do not work with stones, and 'setters' who cut, shape and finally set the precious stones in the mount. Precious jewellery is only produced in very small quantities and is often made as a single and unique piece.

2. Designer/maker – costume and fashion jewellery. The designers use materials such as plastics, resins, titanium, silver, brass, copper, wood and ceramics, either singly or in combinations, to produce relatively inexpensive items determined by the demands of the market which is closely related to the influence of fashion. By using machine production methods the unit cost can be very low and good distribution can often ensure large numbers of items being sold in the shops.

The designers who work in either of these two categories can be self-employed and responsible for the making of a complete piece, or they can work in association with specialist firms who may take over the responsibility for one or more parts of the construction process such as casting. The designers who work in precious metals often sell their work direct to their clients and sometimes work to a particular client's commission. Costume and fashion jewellery designers, however, sometimes sell the prototype design to a manufacturer/retailer who is then responsible for the mass-production and marketing. Alternatively, a designer may undertake to get a large order from a retailer mass-produced.

Employment opportunities for makers of precious jewellery are very limited, but jobs sometimes occur at the major firms. The manufacturing jewellers are traditionally specialised into five main areas of work with the firms providing both a service for the designer/craftsman and producing for the mass market. The areas of work are: casting; engraving; polishing/cleaning/barrelling; stone setting; enamelling.

Workshop treatments

Heat. Jewellers usually require heat to soften or 'anneal' the metal to make it more pliable and to 'silver solder' to join metals. The most usual method for obtaining the necessary heat is to use a mixture of gas and air, provided by a compressor, blowpipe or bellows.

Cleaning. After the annealing or soldering process the metal must be cleaned by submerging it in a solution of acid and water, a process known as 'pickling'. Different metals require different acid solutions for this process. When the metal appears pale and clean it is washed and scrubbed with pumice powder, rinsed and dried. The construction of a piece of jewellery involves several different types of tools:
1. Cutting – saws, drills, files.
2. Shaping and forming – raising, bending, planishing, rolling, wire drawing.
3. Joining – soldering, riveting.

Silversmithing
This is a separate design area, allied to jewellery in that the main materials used are metals but not necessarily silver. Much of the work is closely related to product design, and new materials such as stainless steel have revolutionised the traditional hand processes. Cutlery, once an important area, is now nearly all mass-produced and the substitution of plastics and wood for handles is an example of the changes that have been brought about due to the high cost of labour and the increased cost of materials. The market for traditional silversmithing, such as trophy-making, is very small.

Courses
There are a number of courses available in both jewellery and silversmithing, including courses at the City of Birmingham Polytechnic, City of London Polytechnic, Loughborough College of Art and Design and Sheffield City Polytechnic. Middlesex Polytechnic offers a four-year sandwich course in jewellery and ceramics.

Model-making

Industrial model-makers work on architectural, theatre, film, television, industrial and product models, working with a wide range of materials including wood, metals, plastics and a variety of adhesives. The ability to work accurately on a very small scale, together with both machine and hand craft skills, is required. Model-makers creatively interpret and construct three-dimensional models from two-dimensional drawings. The Medway College of Design at Rochester in Kent has a well-established course in industrial model-making at Higher Diploma level.

Product design

The term 'product design' can be misleading. In relation to art and design it nearly always refers to the surface design or styling of a product. Such designers may work with engineering designers, interior designers and architects in the designing or modification of consumer products, electrical and mechanical machinery, transport systems, telecommunications systems and architecture. There are specific courses in product design, and several of the multidisciplinary three-dimensional courses can lead to work in this area. The Polytechnic of the South Bank in London offers a four-year sandwich course in engineering product design and some engineering designers are themselves qualified product designers, having first obtained an engineering qualification and then specialised in product design at postgraduate level. A knowledge of production methods, aesthetics and ergonomics and the ability to design creatively for a wide range of materials including wood, metals and plastics are essential. A high degree of numeracy and the ability to work with a team of specialists in other disciplines are also important.

Stage design

The number of career opportunities for designers who wish to specialise in this area is very limited and the training opportunities are similarly restricted. Designing for the stage is basically a three-dimensional exercise and includes not only work for the theatre but for opera, ballet, films, television, experimental theatre and community arts projects. Any production, however small, usually involves a team of specialists working under the guidance of a director and can include lighting experts, costume designers, set dressers, make-up experts and the supporting craftsmen such as carpenters and electricians. A creative imagination is essential, combined with a highly developed sense of colour and attention to detail. A knowledge of historical styles and periods and the ability to direct a team of experts is also necessary. Stage designers combine many of the talents of architects, interior designers, display designers and fashion designers.

Visual effects designers

The BBC Visual Effects Department recruits all its design staff from visual effects design assistants already employed within the department. The design assistants construct and operate all types of effects, working in such materials as metals, plastics and wood. Workshop experience, including the operating of machine tools, is required and a thorough understanding of the fundamentals of physics, electricity and chemistry is essential. Students with a background of sculpture, painting, model-making, pyrotechnics and optics, together with the ability to produce good representational drawings and with previous experience in this area of work, are at an advantage. The work can be physically arduous and good health is also required.

2.6 FINE ART

Fine art courses offer an excellent, broad, liberal education in the visual arts. They are, in general, not primarily concerned with the training of potential painters and sculptors, although a very small number of graduates will earn their living in this way. They do, however, provide young people with a unique education and training of the visual senses, and the attitudes and concepts which are learned provide a view of the world and all its activities which are life enhancing and marketable.

Students who are determined to succeed as professional fine artists will probably do so. The State offers no support once the student has left college and this is understandable. Any bureaucracy tends to work towards the *status quo*, and once a fine artist is prepared to compromise in order to survive it is difficult to maintain any integrity. Teaching offers some financial support by the provision of part-time contracts in art and design schools and colleges, but this traditional area of employment is changing due to both economic and demographic changes.

For the minority who have the talent and motivation to succeed as professional artists the support of professional colleagues and friends is often essential. There are no 'rules' or established criteria and this can make the experience both stimulating and isolating. In the early stages the degree of permanence of any work is unimportant. Dissatisfaction with systems of sponsorship such as that of the Arts Council of Great Britain or the influence of commercial dealers through the gallery networks has led many fine artists to explore ways of producing work which is not obviously marketable and in so doing they have changed the nature of the work itself. Nevertheless, the dealers have also adapted to these changes and have encompassed in some form or other many of the art forms that were thought to be impossible to market. Traditional activities such as painting and sculpture periodically recharge themselves, but many fine artists now find their best means of expression through photography, video, film, theatre and community arts. Social and economic changes affect young artists like everyone else and their work merely reflects the world in which we all live. It is important not to have a fixed idea of what is art. This can limit individual creative responses to changing situations.

Scenic artists, Film television

Artists responsible for the painting of backcloths, gauzes and decorative features such as floor designs are known as scenic artists. Such work can also include the representation of carpets, curtains and tapestries and special tasks associated with a particular historical period or style. Art and design school training to diploma level is normally required and the major television companies prefer artists with some previous direct experience of work in theatre, film or television. The number of career opportunities is very limited.

2.7 CONSERVATION

The conservation and restoration of works of art, buildings, furniture, books and documents require particular skills and a knowledge of the history of art, design, architecture and archaeology. Museums and major art galleries probably provide the largest number of career opportunities, but the number of posts is very limited. Specialist courses, such as the Courtauld Institute of Art Diploma in the Conservation of Paintings course or the Paper Conservation course at Camberwell School of Art, provide for professional education and training. The museum service, National Trust, Department of the Environment and other agencies who are responsible for the maintenance and conservation of works of art of all kinds sometimes have specialised departments dealing with this work. Much conservation work is scientifically based and a knowledge of physics and chemistry is often essential for some courses.

2.8 ART AND DESIGN HISTORY

There are a number of career opportunities available for art and design historians as journalists, academics, teachers, museum and gallery staff, conservationists and restorers. The Courtauld Institute of Art specialises in the study of art history and is one of the Senate Institutes of the University of London. It offers courses leading to the award of degree in the history of European Art and applications should be made through UCCA. Degree courses in the history of art are also available at a number of other universities, including Bristol, where it can be combined with the study of a modern language; Cambridge; East Anglia, where it can be combined with the study of literature; and Reading, where it can be combined with the study of art. There are courses in the history of design leading to the award of CNAA degrees at Brighton and Manchester Polytechnics and a course in the history of art and design in the modern period is available at Leicester Polytechnic. The history of modern art, design and film can be studied for a first degree at Newcastle-upon-Tyne Polytechnic and the history of art, design and film at Sheffield City Polytechnic. The North Staffordshire Polytechnic offers a degree course in the history of design and the visual arts. There is a growing interest in the history of design, and the development of BTEC design courses may provide some opportunities for design historians to work alongside practising designers and designers in training.

CHAPTER 3

Visual research

Fig. 3.1 Visual research – BTEC General Art and Design Course students from Barnet College on a Field Study Course at Kilve Court, Somerset

3.1 EDUCATIONAL VISITS

Visits to art galleries, museums and other centres are an important part of the work of many artists and designers. This will often involve travel and a knowledge of sources for research material is, therefore, invaluable.

Discovering a small, specialist museum can be very rewarding and most towns have a local museum with curators who are usually very familiar with their area. Major museums often provide special research facilities for students, including study rooms. Explore local possibilities.

Churches are a rich source for study, particularly for stained glass and carvings. Local cemeteries are a good source for the study of lettering. Many local authorities have parks departments who maintain large greenhouses for growing plants for public spaces: they are often willing to let students work in the greenhouses studying tropical and semi-tropical plants. College and public libraries are another source of research material. The UK national inter-library lending system is the best in the world and it is possible to obtain almost any book from any source. The British Library has a newspaper and periodical library located in North London. Some public libraries have specialist departments and it is always worth consulting the staff about particular interests. There are some useful publications which can be of help. The guide *Museums and Galleries in Great Britain and Ireland* published annually (British Leisure Publications) is an inexpensive and useful reference guide to over 1000 centres. The National Trust publish a guide and map to their houses and gardens which are open to the public. The annual *Historic Houses, Castles and Gardens* guide (British Leisure Publications) lists the majority of both public and privately owned properties open to the public.

If a visit to a National Trust property or a private house is planned, particularly during the summer months, always telephone beforehand and check that making sketches or taking photographs is allowed. It is also worth checking on research facilities for students when visiting museums and galleries. There are strict rules about taking photographs in some museums. Information on ancient monuments and historic buildings which are the responsibility of the Department of the Environment can be obtained from a series of guides published by Her Majesty's Stationery Office.

It is impossible to list all the sources for research. This section of the book identifies some areas which have proved useful. Using one source as a starting-point can lead to the discovery of other, more personal, sources.

Equipment

Some basic equipment is needed. Keep this to a minimum. If an important section of a museum is cluttered up with students and their equipment it makes worthwhile study almost impossible. A camera with a flash is invaluable. Remember to obtain permission before taking photographs indoors. A sketch-book, rather than a sketch-pad, together with a range of drawing materials, inks, a small, leakproof container of water, erasers and a knife for sharpening, should complete a basic kit. All these items can be comfortably carried in a designer's box. Avoid taking a drawing board, but a small, collapsible, stool would be a bonus.

3.2 STUDENT TRAVEL

British Rail

Young Persons Railcard

The British Rail Young Persons Railcard, for which a charge is made, entitles students or anyone under the age of twenty-four to reductions in the price of rail travel but there are special conditions attached to the issue of these tickets. These conditions are periodically changed and you should enquire from your nearest main-line station for information relating to the current conditions. The railcard is valid for one year and normally gives one-third off the price of a standard-class rail ticket for certain journeys and times. This discount can also apply to Off Savers, Network Awaybreaks, Cheap Day Returns, Standard Singles and Standard Returns, Standard Day Returns, Rail Rovers and, in London, half price on the Network Card. The use of some discounted tickets is limited to off-peak travel, but a minimum fare normally operates before 10.00 a.m. on weekdays.

Interrail Card

Certain reductions on Interrail Cards may be available to purchasers of a Young Persons Railcard. Interrail cards provide for one month's unlimited second-class travel on the rail networks of twenty-one European countries including Morocco for anyone under twenty-six. The issue of a railcard requires two copies of a passport-style photograph of yourself and the completion of an application form obtainable from main-line stations.

Coach Travel

Student Coach Card

Student Coach Cards allow discounts of 33 per cent off standard fares throughout Britain on National Express, Scottish Citylink and London Express services. The card also entitles holders to ten per cent reductions off some continental services and to discounts on some other UK services. The card is valid for twelve months. Cards can be obtained from Student Travel Offices or by completing an application form obtainable from Student Coach Card, National Express Ltd, Ensign Court, 4 Vicarage Road, Edgbaston, Birmingham B15 3ES.

Travel in London

London Transport (buses and Underground) do not offer any special student travel facilities. They do, however, offer concessions to all members of the public.

Travelcards. Unlimited travel on bus, Underground and British Rail services as defined by zones and price. Available for seven days, monthly, quarterly or annually.

Off-peak Travelcards.   Also available from 9.30 a.m. Monday to Friday and any time at weekends. Bus Passes can be obtained for unlimited bus travel for seven days, monthly or annually.

One Day Bus Pass.   Available for bus journeys in Inner or Outer London fare zones, at any time of day. For full information on London Regional Transport services telephone 071 222 1234 at any time – day or night. Free timetables and leaflets can be obtained by writing to Travel Information, 55 Broadway, London, SW1H 0BD.

3.3 RESEARCH CENTRES

Ceramics, glass

Bedford   Cecil Higgins Art Gallery, Castle Close. Open weekdays (except Mondays) 12.30 p.m. to 5.00 p.m. Tel: 0234 211222

Brighton   Brighton Museum, Church Street. Open Tuesdays to Saturdays 10.00 a.m. to 5.45 p.m. Admission free. Tel: 0273 603005

Cheltenham   Cheltenham Museum, Clarence Street. Open Mondays to Saturdays 10.00 a.m. to 5.30 p.m. Admission free. Tel: 0242 37431

Durham   Gulbenkian Museum of Oriental Art and Archaeology, Elvet Hill. Open Mondays to Fridays 9.30 a.m. to 1.00 p.m. and 2.15 p.m. to 5.00 p.m. Admission charge. Tel: 0385 66711

London   Percival David Foundation of Chinese Art (Chinese Ceramics), 53 Gordon Square, WC1H 0PD. Open Mondays 2.00 p.m. to 5.00 p.m. Tuesdays to Fridays 10.30 a.m. to 5.00 p.m. and Saturdays 10.30 a.m. to 1.00 p.m. Tel: 071 387 3909
    The British Museum and the Victoria and Albert Museum have important collections of china and glass. For details of opening times see under Design and Fine art.

Nottingham   Nottingham Castle Museum. Open daily from 10.00 a.m. Admission free. Tel: 0602 41188

St Helens   Pilkington Glass Museum, Prescot Road. Open Mondays to Fridays 10.00 a.m. to 5.00 p.m., Saturdays and Sundays 2.00 p.m. to 4.30 p.m. Admission free. Tel: 0744 28882

Stoke-on-Trent   City Museum, Bethesda Street, Hanley. Open weekdays 10.30 a.m. to 5.00 p.m. Admission free. Tel: 0782 202173

    Gladstone Pottery Museum, Uttoxeter Road, Longton. Open

according to season 10.30 a.m. to 3.30 p.m. Closed Mondays from
October to March. Admission charge. Tel: 0782 319232

See also the Fitzwilliam Museum, Cambridge (Fine Art Section) and the
Ashmolean Museum, Oxford (Fine Art Section). The majority of
national and regional museums have important collections of ceramics
and glass.

Costume

Bath   Museum of Costume, Assembly Rooms. Open – Winter –
Mondays to Saturdays 10.00 a.m. to 5.00 p.m., Sundays 11.00 a.m. to
5.00 p.m. Summer – Mondays to Saturdays 9.30 a.m. to 6.00 p.m.
Admission charge. Tel: 0225 61111

Castle Howard, York   Castle Howard Costume Galleries, Castle
Howard, York. Open daily from Easter to October 11.30 a.m. to
5.00 p.m. Admission charge. Tel: Coneysthorpe 333

Manchester   The Gallery of English Costume, Platt Hall, Platt Fields,
Rusholme. Open weekdays 10 a.m. to 6.00 p.m., Sundays 2.00 p.m. to
6.00 p.m. Closed from November to February. Tel: 061 224 5217

Nottingham   Museum of Costume and Textiles, Castlegate. Open daily
10.00 a.m. to 5.00 p.m. Admission free. Tel: 0602 411881

See also the Victoria and Albert Museum, which has a major collection
of costumes (see Design section), and the collections of other major
national and regional museums. The museums of the armed services
have collections of military uniforms and the armour collections at the
Tower of London are excellent (see Military section). Costume research
can also be carried out by studying paintings of various periods. The
collections at the Rangers House, Blackheath; Montacute House,
Yeovil, and the National Portrait Gallery (see Fine Art) may be
particularly useful.

Crafts (including ethnological collections)

Bath   The American Museum in Britain, Claverton Manor, near Bath.
Normally open from April to October daily (except Mondays) from
2.00 p.m. to 5.00 p.m. Education Department. Tel: 0225 63538
Admission charge.

Hull   Town Docks Museum, Queen Victoria Square. Open weekdays
10.00 a.m. to 5.00 p.m. Admission free. Tel: 0482 222737

Liverpool   Liverpool Museum, William Brown Street. Open weekdays 10.00 a.m. to 5.00 p.m. Admission free. Tel: 051 207 0001

London   Bethnal Green Museum (a branch of the Victoria and Albert Museum). Open Mondays to Thursdays 10.00 a.m. to 6.00 p.m., Saturdays 10.00 a.m. to 6.00 p.m. Sundays 2.30 p.m. to 6.00 p.m. Museum of childhood. Admission free. Tel: 081 980 2415

Fenton House, Hampstead Grove, Hampstead, NW3. Collection of early musical instruments. Open Wednesdays to Sundays 2.00 p.m. to 6.00 p.m. Admission charge. Tel: 071 435 3471

Horniman Museum, London Road, Forest Hill, SE23 3PQ. Open Mondays to Saturdays 10.30 a.m. to 6.00 p.m. Admission free. Tel: 081 699 2339

Museum of Mankind, 6, Burlington Gardens, W1X 2EX (Ethnological Collection of the British Museum). Open weekdays 10.00 a.m. to 5.00 p.m., Sundays 2.30 p.m. to 6.00 p.m. Admission free. Tel: 071 437 2224

Northleach, Gloucestershire   Cotswold Countryside Collection, Fosseway. Open during the summer months. Weekdays 10.00 a.m. to 6.00 p.m., Sundays 2.00 p.m. to 6.00 p.m. Admission charge. Tel: 0285 5611

Oxford   Pitt-Rivers Museum, South Parks Road. Open Mondays to Saturdays 2.00 p.m. to 4.00 p.m. Admission free. Tel: 0865 270927

Reading   Museum of English Rural Life (University of Reading), Whiteknights, Reading (Fig. 3.2). Open Tuesdays to Fridays 10.00 a.m. to 4.30 p.m. Saturdays 10.00 a.m. to 1.00 p.m. and 2.00 p.m. to 4.30 p.m. Admission free. Permanent exhibition of agricultural tools and implements, rural industries and domestic equipment, together with a collection of farm wagons and ploughs. The photographic library contains more than 250,000 prints and negatives from the mid-nineteenth century to the present day. Tel: 0734 875123

St Fagans, South Glamorgan Wales   Welsh Folk Museum, St Fagans Castle. Open weekdays 10.00 a.m. to 5.00 p.m., Sundays 2.30 p.m. to 5.00 p.m. Admission charge. Tel: 0222 569441

Stocksfield, Northumberland (14 miles west of Newcastle)   National Tractor and Farm Museum, Newton near Stocksfield. Open daily 10.00 a.m. to 6.00 p.m. Admission charge. Museum of the Year 1981. Major exhibition of farm tractors, farming bygones, static engines and farm trades. Also known as the Hunday Museum. Tel: 0661 842553

York   York Castle Museum, Eye of York, YO1 1RY. Open according

Fig. 3.2   Museum of English Rural Life – Reading, Domestic Section

to season. Mondays to Saturdays from 9.30 a.m. Sundays from 10.00 a.m. Admission charge. Tel: 0904 653611

Design

Brighton   The Royal Pavilion, Regency Palace and Exhibition. Open daily 10.00 a.m. to 5.00 p.m. (late opening to 7.30 p.m. during July, August and September). Admission charge. Tel: 0273 603005

London   Clockmakers' Company Museum, Guildhall Library, Aldermanbury Street, EC2P 2EJ. Open Mondays to Fridays 9.30 a.m. to 5.00 p.m. Admission free. Tel: 071 606 3030

The Design Centre, 28 Haymarket, SW1. Continually changing display of British-made goods. Excellent design bookshop. Open Mondays to Saturdays 9.00 a.m. to 8.00 p.m. Admission free. Tel: 071 839 8000

Design Museum, Butlers Wharf, Shad Thames, London SE1 2YD. Open Tuesdays to Sundays 11.30 a.m. to 6.30 p.m. Closed Mondays. Admission charge. Tel: 071 403 6933

Goldsmiths' Hall, Foster Lane, Cheapside, EC2. The collection of the Goldsmiths' Company. Tel: 071 606 8971 for special permission to study the collection.

Geffrye Museum, Kingsland Road, Shoreditch, E2 8EA. Exhibition of period rooms from about 1600. Excellent examples of furniture. Open Tuesdays to Saturdays 10.00 a.m. to 5.00 p.m., Sundays 2.00 p.m. to 5.00 p.m. Admission free. Tel: 071 739 8368

Leighton House, 12 Holland Park Road, Kensington, W14. A good example of High Victorian interior design. Open daily 11.00 a.m. to 5.00 p.m. Tel: 071 602 3316

National Film Archive, 81 Dean Street, W1. Open 10.00 a.m. to 6.00 p.m. Tel: 071 437 4355 for appointment. Not open to the general public.

National Postal Museum, King Edward building, King Edward Street, EC1. Major display of postage stamps. Photograph service. Research facilities. Library. Open Mondays to Fridays 10.00 a.m. to 4.30 p.m. Tel: 071 432 3851

Pollocks' Toy Museum, 1 Scala Street, W1P 1LT. Open Mondays to Saturdays 10.00 a.m. to 5.00 p.m. Admission charge. Tel: 071 636 3452

Royal Botanic Gardens (Kew Gardens). Open according to season from 10.00 a.m. Admission charge.

Science Museum, Exhibition Road, South Kensington. Open weekdays 10.00 a.m. to 6.00 p.m., Sundays 2.30 p.m. to 6.00 p.m. Admission charge. Tel: 071 589 3456

Victoria and Albert Museum, Cromwell road, South Kensington, SW7. Open Mondays to Thursdays and Saturdays 10.00 a.m. to 5.50 p.m., Sundays 2.30 p.m. to 5.50 p.m. Admission charge. Tel: 071 589 6371

William Morris Gallery, Water House, Lloyd Park, Forest Road, Walthamstow, E17. Open weekdays 10.00 a.m. to 5.00 p.m. Tel: 081 527 5544

Manchester   Museum of Science and Industry, Liverpool Road, Castleford, Manchester. Open every day 10.00 a.m. to 5.00 p.m. Admission charge. Tel: 061 832 2244

The Manchester Museum, The University, Oxford Road, Manchester M13 9PL. Open Mondays to Saturdays 10.00 a.m. to 5.00 p.m. Tel: 061 273 3333

---

*Fig. 3.3   (a)   Museum Study at British Museum by BTEC General Art and Design
Course students – Barnet College*
*(b)   Museum Study of Ceramics of BTEC General Art and Design Course
students – Barnet College*

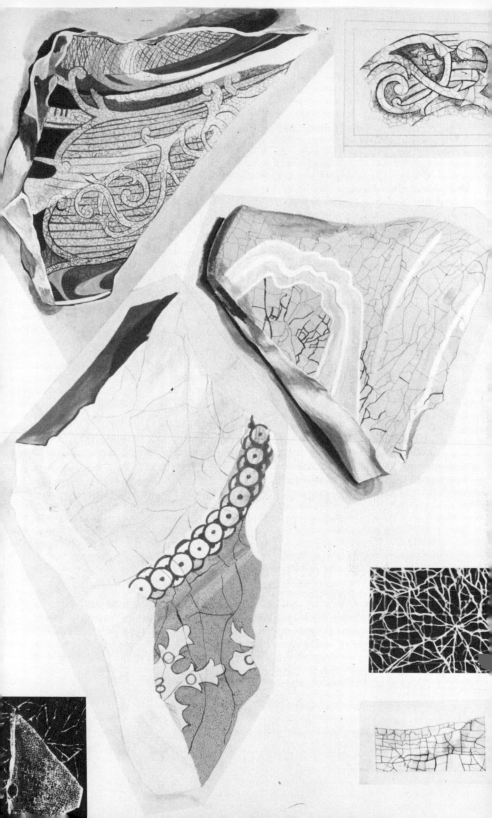

Northampton Central Museum Footwear Exhibition, Guildhall Road. Open Mondays to Saturdays 10.00 a.m. to 6.00 p.m. Admission free. Tel: 0604 34881

Rothbury, Northumberland Cragside, near Rothbury. House modified by the architect Norman Shaw and containing excellent examples of Victorian interiors. Open daily during the summer months 1.00 p.m. to 6.00 p.m. Closed on Mondays. Admission charge. Tel: 0669 20333

Street, Somerset Street Shoe Museum (C. & C. Clark Ltd), High Street. Open (by appointment) to students for study all the year. Open to the public from May to October. A large and comprehensive collection of shoes and related items from Roman and through medieval times to the present day. The collection includes costume illustrations, fashion plates and cartoons from the eighteenth century onwards. Admission free. Tel: 0458 43131

The majority of national and regional museums have substantial collections of items which can provide excellent reference material for the study of all aspects of design.

Fine arts

This section includes public galleries and museums that have both permanent collections and temporary exhibitions on display and commercial or grant-aided galleries that regularly exhibit contemporary work. Details of current exhibitions can be obtained from the national and local press as well as from specialist art and design magazines. N.B. In this section only galleries that have changing exhibitions are marked with an asterisk*.

Belfast Ulster Museum, Botanic Gardens, Belfast, BT9 5AB. Open weekdays 10.00 a.m. to 5.00 p.m., Sundays 2.30 p.m. to 5.30 p.m. Admission free. Tel: 0232 668251

Birmingham Museum and Art Gallery, Chamberlain Square, Birmingham, B3 3DH. Open Mondays to Saturdays 10.00 a.m. to 5.30 p.m., Sundays 2.00 p.m. to 5.30 p.m. Admission free. Tel: 021 235 2834. Education Department Tel: 021 235 3890

Ikon Gallery,* John Bright Street.

Bournemouth Russell-Cotes Art Gallery, East Cliff.

Bradford Art Gallery and Museum, Cartwright Hall. Open Tuesdays to Saturdays 10.00 a.m. to 5.00 p.m. Admission free. Tel: 0274 493313

Brighton Axis Gallery,* 12 Market Street, The Lanes.

Burstow Gallery, Brighton College,* Eastern Road.

Barclaycraft Gallery,* 7, East Street. Gardner Centre Gallery,* University of Sussex.

Bristol Arnolfini Art Centre,* Narrow Quay, Bristol, BS1 4QA. Tel: 0272 299191

Cambridge Fitzwilliam Museum, Trumpington Street. Open Tuesdays to Saturdays. Lower Galleries, Ceramics, etc. 10.00 a.m. to 2.00 p.m. Upper Galleries, Fine Art, 2.00 p.m. to 5.00 p.m. Admission free. Tel: 0223 69501/3

Kettles Yard Gallery,* Northampton Street. Open daily 12.30 p.m. to 5.30 p.m., Sundays 2.00 p.m. to 5.30 p.m. Tel: 0223 352124

Cardiff National Museum of Wales. Open weekdays 10.00 a.m. to 5.00 p.m., Sundays 2.30 p.m. to 5.00 p.m. Tel: 0222 397951

Colchester Minories Gallery,* 74 High Street.

Dublin National Gallery of Ireland, Merrion Square. Open weekdays 10.00 a.m. to 6.00 p.m., Sundays 2.00 p.m. to 5.00 p.m. Tel: Dublin 767571

Hugh Lane Gallery of Modern Art, Charlement House, Parnell Square. Open weekdays Tuesdays to Saturdays 9.30 a.m. to 6.00 p.m. Sundays 11.00 a.m. to 2.00 p.m. Tel: Dublin 741903

Durham Bowes Museum, Barnard Castle. Open Mondays to Saturdays according to season from 10.00 a.m., Sundays from 2.00 p.m. Admission charge. Tel: 0833 37139

Eastbourne Tower Art Gallery,* Borough Lane.

Edinburgh City Art Centre,* 1–4 Market Street. Open weekdays 10.00 a.m. to 5.00 p.m. Admission free. Tel: 031 225 2424

Fruit Market Gallery,* 29 Market Street. Open weekdays 10.00 a.m. to 5.30 p.m. Tel: 031 226 2883

National Gallery of Scotland, The Mound, Edinburgh, EH2 2EL. Open weekdays 10.00 a.m. to 5.00 p.m., Sundays 2.00 p.m. to 5.00 p.m. Admission free. Tel: 031 556 8921

Fig. 3.4 Visual research study – Foundation Course student – Barnet College

Royal Museum of Scotland, Chambers Street, Edinburgh, EH1 1JF. Open weekdays 10.00 a.m. to 5.00 p.m., Sundays 2.00 p.m. to 5.00 p.m. Admission free. Tel: 031 225 7534

Scottish National Gallery of Modern Art, Bedford Road, Edinburgh, EH4 3DR. Open weekdays 10.00 a.m. to 5.00 p.m., Sundays 2.00 p.m. to 5.00 p.m. Admission free. Tel: 031 556 8921

Scottish National Portrait Gallery, Queen Street, EH2 1JD. Open weekdays 10.00 a.m. to 5.00 p.m., Sundays 2.00 p.m. to 5.00 p.m. Admission free. Tel: 031 556 8921

Glasgow   Art Gallery and Museum, Kelvingrove. Open weekdays 10.00 a.m. to 5.00 p.m., Sundays 2.00 p.m. to 5.00 p.m. Admission free. Tel: 041 357 3929

The Burrell Collection, Pollok Country Park, G43 1AT. Open weekdays 10.00 a.m. to 5.00 p.m., Sundays 2.00 p.m. to 5.00 p.m. Tel: 041 649 7151

Hunterian Collection Art Gallery, University of Glasgow, Hillhead Street. Open Mondays to Fridays 10.00 a.m. to 5.00 p.m., Saturdays 9.30 a.m. to 1.00 p.m. Tel: 041 330 4221

Hull   Ferens Art Gallery, Queen Victoria Square. Open weekdays 10.00 a.m. to 5.00 p.m. Admission free. Tel: 0482 222750

Leeds   Leeds City Art Gallery. Open weekdays 10.00 a.m. to 6.00 p.m., Sundays 2.00 p.m. to 5.00 p.m. Admission free. Tel: 0532 462495

Leicester   Leicestershire Museum and Art Gallery, New Walk. Open weekdays 10.00 a.m. to 5.30 p.m. Admission free. Tel: 0533 554100

Liverpool   Tate Gallery Liverpool, Albert Dock, L3 4BB. Open Tuesdays to Sundays 11.00 a.m. to 7.00 p.m. Closed Mondays. Tel: 051 709 3223

Walker Art Gallery, William Brown Street. Open weekdays 10.00 a.m. to 5.00 p.m. Tel: 051 207 0001

London   Air Gallery,★ 6/8 Rosebery Avenue, EC1. Open Mondays to Fridays 11.00 a.m. to 6.00 p.m., Saturdays 11.00 a.m. to 2.00 p.m. Tel: 071 287 7751

Agnew and Sons, 43 Old Bond Street, W1 Tel: 071 629 6176

Angela Flowers Gallery,★ 11 Tottenham Mews, W1. Open Mondays to Fridays 10.30 a.m. to 5.30 p.m., Saturdays 10.30 a.m. to 12.30 p.m. Tel: 071 637 3089

Annely Juda Fine Art, 11 Tottenham Mews, W1. Tel: 071 637 5517

Anthony d'Offay, 9 and 23 Dering Street, W1. Tel: 071 499 4100

British Museum, Great Russell Street, W1. Open weekdays 10.00 a.m. to 5.00 p.m., Sundays 2.30 p.m. to 6.00 p.m. Admission free. Tel: 071 636 1555

Browse & Darby,* 19 Cork Street, W1. Open Mondays to Fridays 10.00 a.m. to 5.30 p.m. Tel: 071 734 7984

Buckingham Palace – The Queen's Gallery, Buckingham Palace Road, SW1. Open Tuesday to Saturdays 11.00 a.m. to 5.00 p.m., Sundays 2.00 p.m. to 5.00 p.m. Admission charge.

Camden Arts Centre,* Arkwright Road, Finchley Road, NW3. Open Mondays to Saturdays 11.00 a.m. to 6.00 p.m.. Tel: 071 435 2643

Courtauld Institute Galleries, Woburn Square, W1. Open weekdays 10.00 a.m. to 5.00 p.m., Sundays 2.00 p.m. to 5.00 p.m. Admission charge. Tel: 071 580 1015

Crane Kalman, 178 Brompton Road, SW3. Tel: 071 584 7566

Curwen Gallery, 4 Windmill Street, W1. Tel: 071 636 1459

Drian Gallery,* 7 Porchester Place, W2. Open Mondays to Fridays 10.00 a.m. to 5.00 p.m., Saturdays 10.00 a.m. to 1.00 p.m. Tel: 071 723 9473

Dulwich Picture Gallery, College Road, SE21. Open Tuesdays to Saturdays 10.00 a.m. to 5.00 p.m., Sundays 2.00 p.m. to 5.00 p.m. Admission free. Tel: 081 693 5254

Fischer Fine Art,* 30 King Street, St James's, SW1. Open Mondays to Fridays 10.00 a.m. to 5.30 p.m., Saturdays 10.00 a.m. to 12.30 p.m. Tel: 071 839 3942

Gimpel Fils,* 30 Davies Street, W1. Open Mondays to Fridays 9.30 a.m. to 5.30 p.m., Saturdays 10.00 a.m. to 1.00 p.m. Tel: 071 493 2488

Goethe Institute,* 50 Princes Gate, Exhibition Road, SW7. Tel: 071 581 3344

Hayward Gallery, Belvedere Road, South Bank, SE1. For details of temporary exhibitions see national press or telephone 071 928 3144

Institute of Contemporary Arts (ICA),* Nash House, The Mall, SW1. For details of temporary exhibitions and theatre/film programmes telephone 071 930 0493. Theatre box office Tel: 071 930 3647

Iveagh Bequest, Kenwood, Hampstead Lane, NW3. Open daily 10.00 a.m. to 5.00 p.m. Admission free. Tel: 081 348 1286

Knoedler Gallery,* 22 Cork Street, W1. Open Mondays to Fridays 10.00 a.m. to 5.00 p.m., Saturdays 10.00 a.m. to 1.00 p.m. Tel: 071 439 1096

Lisson Gallery, 67 Lisson Street, NW1. Open Mondays to Fridays 10.00 a.m. to 6.00 p.m., Saturdays 10.00 a.m. to 1.00 p.m. Tel: 071 724 2739

Marlborough Fine Art,* 6 Albemarle Street, W1. Open Mondays to Fridays 10.00 a.m. to 6.00 p.m., Saturdays 10.00 a.m. to 12.30 p.m. Tel: 071 629 5161

Mayor Rowan Gallery, 31A Bruton Place, W1. Tel: 071 499 3011

Mercury Gallery,* 26 Cork Street, W1. Open Mondays to Fridays 10.00 a.m. to 5.30 p.m., Saturdays 10.00 a.m. to 12.30 p.m. Tel: 071 734 7800

National Gallery, Trafalgar Square, WC2. Open weekdays 10.00 a.m. to 6.00 p.m., Sundays 2.00 p.m. to 6.00 p.m. Admission free. Tel: 071 839 3321

National Portrait Gallery, St Martin's Place, Trafalgar Square, WC2. Open Mondays to Fridays 10.00 a.m. to 5.00 p.m., Saturdays 10.00 a.m. to 6.00 p.m., Sundays 2.00 p.m. to 6.00 p.m. Admission free. Tel: 071 930 1552

New Art Centre,* 41 Sloane Street, SW1. Open Mondays to Fridays 10.00 a.m. to 6.00 p.m., Saturdays 10.00 a.m. to 1.00 p.m. Tel: 071 235 5844

Nicola Jacobs, 9 Cork Street, W1. Tel: 071 437 3868

Nigel Greenwood Gallery, 4 New Burlington Street, W1. Open Mondays to Fridays. Tel: 071 434 3795

Piccadilly Gallery,* 16 Cork Street, W1. Open Mondays to Fridays 10.00 a.m. to 5.30 p.m. Tel: 071 629 2875

Rangers House, Chesterfield Walk, Blackheath, SE10. Open daily 10.00 a.m. to 5.00 p.m. (winter months 10.00 a.m. to 4.00 p.m.). Admission free. Tel: 081 853 0035

Redfern Gallery,* 20 Cork Street, W1. Open daily Mondays to Fridays 10.00 a.m. to 5.30 p.m. Tel: 071 734 1732

Royal Academy of Arts, Piccadilly, W1. Loan exhibitions throughout the year. Open daily 10.00 a.m. to 6.00 p.m. For details see national press or telephone 071 734 9052

Saatchi Collection, 98A Boundary Road, NW8. Tel: 071 624 8299

Serpentine Gallery, Kensington Gardens, W2. Temporary exhibitions of contemporary art. Opening times vary according to the season starting at 10.00 a.m. each weekday. Admission free. For details see national press or telephone 071 402 6075

Sir John Soane's Museum, 13 Lincoln's Inn Fields, WC2. Open Tuesdays to Saturdays, 10.00 a.m. to 5.00 p.m. Tel: 071 406 2107

Tate Gallery, Millbank, SW1. Open weekdays 10.00 a.m. to 6.00 p.m., Sundays 2.00 p.m. to 6.00 p.m. Admission free. Tel: 071 821 1313. For details of special exhibitions recorded information is available on 071 821 7128

Waddington Galleries Ltd, 11 and 34 Cork Street, W1. Open Mondays to Fridays 10.00 a.m. to 5.30 p.m., Saturdays 10.00 a.m. to 1.00 p.m. Tel: 071 437 8611

Waddington Graphics, 2 and 4 Cork Street, W1. Tel: 071 439 1866

Wallace Collection, Hertford House, Manchester Square, W1. Open weekdays 10.00 a.m. to 5.00 p.m., Sundays 2.00 p.m. to 5.00 p.m. Tel: 071 935 0687

Whitechapel Art Gallery, Whitechapel High Street, E1. Temporary exhibitions of contemporary art. Open daily (except Saturdays) 11.00 a.m. to 6.00 p.m. For details telephone 071 377 0107

Manchester   The City Art Gallery, Mosley Street, M2 3JL. Open weekdays 10.00 a.m. to 6.00 p.m. Admission free. Tel: 061 236 9422

Athenaeum Gallery, Princess Street. Open weekdays 10.00 a.m. to 6.00 p.m. Tel: 061 236 9422

Whitworth Art Gallery, Oxford Road. Open weekdays 10.00 a.m. to 5.00 p.m. Admission free. Tel: 061 273 4865

Newcastle upon Tyne   Laing Art Gallery, Higham Place. Open Mondays to Saturdays 10.00 a.m. to 6.00 p.m., Sundays 2.30 p.m. to 5.30 p.m. Admission free. Tel: 0632 327734

The Hatton Gallery, The Quadrangle. Open weekdays 10.00 a.m. to 5.30 p.m. Admission free. Tel. 091 2328511

Norwich   Norwich Castle Museum, NR1 3JV. Open weekdays 10.00 a.m. to 5.00 p.m., Sundays 2.00 p.m. to 5.00 p.m. Admission charge. Tel: 0603 611277

Sainsbury Centre for the Visual Arts, University of East Anglia, NR4 7TJ. Open daily except Mondays 12.00 noon to 5.00 p.m. Tel: 0603 56060

Oxford   The Ashmolean Museum, Beaumont Street. Open Mondays to Saturdays 10.00 a.m. to 4.00 p.m., Sundays 2.00 p.m. to 4.00 p.m. Admission free. Tel: 0865 278000

Museum of Modern Art, Pembroke Street. Open Tuesdays to Saturdays 10.00 a.m. to 5.00 p.m., Sundays 2.00 p.m. to 5.00 p.m. Admission free. Tel: 0865 722733

Plymouth City Art Gallery, Drake Circus. Open weekdays 10.00 a.m. to 6.00 p.m. Admission free. Tel: 0752 264878

St Ives Barbara Hepworth Museum, Barnoon Hill. Open weekdays 10.00 a.m. to 5.30 p.m. during the spring and summer. The museum closes at 4.30 p.m. during the winter months. Admission charge. Tel: 0736 796226

Sheffield Graves Art Gallery, Surrey Street. Open weekdays 10.00 a.m. to 5.00 p.m. Admission free. Tel: 0742 734781

Mappin Art Gallery, Weston Park. Open weekdays 10.00 a.m. to 5.00 p.m., Sundays 2.00 p.m. to 5.00 p.m. Admission free. Tel: 0742 26281

Southampton Art Gallery, Civic Centre. Open weekdays 11.00 a.m. to 5.45 p.m., Sundays 2.00 p.m. to 5.00 p.m. Admission free. Tel: 0703 832769

Wakefield Art Gallery, Wentworth Terrace. Open weekdays 12.30 p.m. to 5.30 p.m., Sundays 2.30 p.m. to 5.30 p.m. Admission free. Tel: 0924 370211

Yorkshire Sculpture Park, Bretton Hall College, West Bretton, near Wakefield. Major exhibition of sculpture in an outdoor setting. Easy access from the M1, junction 38. Open Mondays to Fridays 10.00 a.m. to 6.00 p.m., Saturdays and Sundays 10.00 a.m. to 4.00 p.m. Admission charge. Tel: 092 485 261

Wolverhampton Central Art Gallery, Lichfield Street. Open Mondays to Saturdays 10.00 a.m. to 6.00 p.m. Admission free. Tel: 0902 312032

Yeovil Montacute House, Montacute, TA15 6XP (National Portrait Gallery Exhibition of Elizabethan and Jacobean Portraits). Open from April to October daily except Tuesdays from 12.30 p.m. to 6.00 p.m. Admission charge. Tel: 0935 823289

York City Art Gallery, Exhibition Square. Open weekdays 10.00 a.m. to 5.00 p.m., Sundays 2.30 p.m. to 5.00 p.m. Admission charge. Tel: 0904 623829

Industry

Amberley   Chalk Pits Museum, Houghton Bridge, Amberley, West Sussex. A 14.5 ha (36-acre) open-air centre for industrial history. Open from Easter to October, Wednesdays to Sundays 11.00 a.m. to 6.00 p.m. Admission charge. Tel: 079 881 370

Beamish, Co. Durham   North of England Open Air Museum. A 81 ha (200-acre) site containing reconstructions of buildings, a colliery, railway and farm, using the original materials and equipment. Open from April to September daily 10.00 a.m. to 6.00 p.m. From October to March the museum is closed on Mondays but open on other days 10.00 a.m. to 5.00 p.m. Admission charge. Tel: 0207 231811

Bristol   Bristol Industrial Museum, Prince's Wharf, Bristol 2. Open Mondays to Wednesdays and Saturdays and Sundays 10.00 a.m. to 12.00 noon and 1.00 p.m. to 5.00 p.m. Tel: 0272 299711

Stoke-on-Trent   Chatterley Whitfield Mining Museum, Chatterley Whitfield Colliery, Turnstall, ST6 8UN. Open Tuesdays to Fridays 9.30 a.m. to 4.30 p.m., Saturdays and Sundays 10.00 a.m. to 5.00 p.m. Admission charge. Tel: 0782 813337

Styal, Cheshire   Quarry Bank Mill. Open according to season, but normally Tuesdays to Sundays from 11.00 a.m. Admission charge. Tel: 0625 527468

Telford   Ironbridge Gorge Museum (Fig. 3.5). A major museum covering the period of the Industrial Revolution, spread over seven sites including a 42-acre open-air museum. Admission charges. Tel: 095 245 3522

Ulster   Ulster Folk and Transport Museum, Cultra Manor, Holywood BT18 0UE, Northern Ireland. A major folk and transport museum on a site of 178 acres about 13 km (8 miles) from Belfast. From May to September open weekdays 11.00 a.m. to 7.00 p.m., Sundays 2.00 p.m. to 7.00 p.m. From October to April the museum is open weekdays 11.00 a.m. to 5.00 p.m., Sundays 2.00 p.m. to 5.00 p.m. Admission charge. Tel: Holywood 5611

Military

Bovington – Wareham   The Tank Museum, Bovington Camp, Wareham, Dorset. Open weekdays 10.00 a.m. to 12.30 p.m. and 2.00 p.m. to 4.45 p.m. Tel: 0929 462721

Duxford, Cambridge   Duxford Airfield, Duxford (a branch of the

Imperial War Museum). Large collection of aircraft including Concorde. Open March to November daily 11.00 a.m. to 5.00 p.m. Admission charge. Tel: 0223 833963

London HMS *Belfast*, Symons Wharf, Vine Lane, SE1. Open daily summer 11.00 a.m. to 5.50 p.m., winter 11.00 a.m. to 4.30 p.m. Admission charge. Tel: 071 407 6434

Imperial War Museum, Lambeth Road, SE1. Open daily 10.00 a.m. to 5.50 p.m., Sundays 2.00 p.m. to 5.50 p.m. Tel: 071 735 8922

The Museum of Artillery, Rotunda, Repository Road, Woolwich, SE18 4JJ. Open from April to October. Mondays to Fridays 10.00 a.m. to 12.45 p.m. and 2.00 p.m. to 5.00 p.m., Saturdays 10.00 a.m. to 12.00 noon and 2.00 p.m. to 5.00 p.m., Sundays 2.00 p.m. to 5.00 p.m. Admission free. Tel: 081 854 2242

National Army Museum, Royal Hospital Road, SW3. Open weekdays 10.00 a.m. to 5.30 p.m., Sundays 2.00 p.m. to 5.30 p.m. Admission free. Tel: 071 730 0717

Royal Air Force Museum, Aerodrome Road, Hendon, NW9. Open weekdays 10.00 a.m. to 6.00 p.m., Sundays 2.00 p.m. to 6.00 p.m. Major exhibition of aircraft. Tel: 081 205 2266

Tower of London, Tower Hill, EC3. Open according to season, weekdays from 9.30 a.m. and Sundays from 2.00 p.m. Admission charge. Tel: 071 709 0765

Wellington Museum, Apsley House, Hyde Park Corner, W1. Open Tuesdays to Thursdays and Saturdays 10.00 a.m. to 6.00 p.m., Sundays 2.30 p.m. to 6.00 p.m. Tel: 071 499 5676

Portsmouth The Royal Naval Museum, HM Naval Base. Open weekdays 10.30 a.m. to 5.30 p.m., Sundays 1.00 p.m. to 5.00 p.m. Admission charge. Tel: 0705 733060

Wolverhampton RAF Aerospace Museum, Royal Air Force Cosford, WV7 3EX. Open Easter to October on Saturdays and Sundays 10.00 a.m. to 5.00 p.m. Admission charge. Tel: Albrighton 4872

Yeovilton Fleet Air Arm/Concorde Museum. Open weekdays 10.00 a.m. to 5.30 p.m., Sundays 12.30 p.m. to 5.30 p.m. Admission charge. Tel: Ilchester 840551

Photography/Film/Television

Bradford National Museum of Photography Film and Television, Prince's View, Bradford, West Yorkshire BE5 0TR. Open weekdays Tuesdays to Sundays 11.00 a.m. to 6.00 p.m. Closed Mondays.

Exhibition Gallery, Museum Shop and Box Office open Tuesdays to Sundays 11.00 a.m. to 7.30 a.m. Films each evening at 7.30 p.m. Tel: 031 (0274) 727488

Cardiff The Photographic Gallery, 31 Charles Street. Tel: 0222 41667

London Museum of the Moving Image (MOMI), South Bank, SE1 8XT. Open Tuesdays to Saturdays 10.00 a.m. to 8.00 p.m., Sundays 10.00 a.m. to 6.00 p.m. Admission charge. Tel: 071 928 3535 (Booking enquiries 071 928 3232)

Kodak Photographic Gallery, 190 High Holborn, WC1. Tel: 071 405 7841

The Photographers Gallery, 5/8 Great Newport Street, WC2. Tel: 071 831 1722

Historic collections of photographs are held by a number of museums and institutions including the Victoria and Albert Museum, London, the National Portrait Gallery, London, the Science Museum, London and the Royal Photographic Society, London.

Sale-rooms

Good sources of material for visual research are available on viewing days at the major art auctioneers' sale-rooms in London and the provinces. Admission is free and special viewing days are set aside for particular groups of items such as jewellery, books, paintings, drawings and furniture. The two leading international auctioneers, Christie's and Sotheby's, both publish excellent illustrated catalogues.

Christie's 8 King Street, St James's, London, SW1Y 6QT. Tel: 071 839 9060. Christie's was founded in 1766 and has sales of Old-Master pictures, water-colours, drawings and prints, impressionist pictures, clocks and watches, coins and medals, furniture, Chinese and Japanese works of art, silver, English and European ceramics and glass, jewellery and books, manuscripts and autograph letters. A free valuation and an expert opinion is available on works of art brought to the reception desk. The premises at 85 Old Brompton Road, South Kensington, SW7 3JS, Tel: 071 581 2231, specialise in lower-price-range items and in collecting fields such as nineteenth- and twentieth-century photographs, cigarette cards, dolls, toys and costumes.

Sotheby's 34–35 New Bond Street, W1A 2AA. Tel: 071 493 8080. Information on London sales is published in the national press.

Fig. 3.5   Ironbridge Gorge Museum – Museum of Iron Foundry Section

Transport

Aysgarth, North Yorkshire   The Yorkshire Museum of Carriages and Horse Drawn Vehicles, York Mills, Aysgarth Falls. Open Easter to October. Daily 10.00 a.m. to 12.00 noon and 2.00 p.m. to 6.00 p.m. Admission charge.

Beaulieu   National Motor Museum, Beaulieu, Hampshire. Open weekdays and Sundays 10.00 a.m. to 6.00 p.m. Admission charge. Tel: 0590 612345

Castle Donnington   The Donnington Collection Single-seater Grand Prix racing cars. Open daily 10.00 a.m. to 6.00 p.m. Admission charge. Tel: 0332 810048

Crich, nr Matlock   The Tramways Museum. Open April to October on Saturdays and Sundays 10.30 a.m. to 5.00 p.m. From June to August also open on Tuesdays, Wednesdays and Thursdays 10.00 a.m. to 4.30 p.m.

Coventry   The Museum of British Road Transport, Cooks Street. Major exhibition of cycles, motor cycles, cars and commercial vehicles. The museum's policy is to maintain all the exhibits in full working order. Open Tuesdays to Fridays 10.00 a.m. to 5.00 p.m., Saturdays 10.00 a.m. to 6.00 p.m. and Sundays 12.00 noon to 6.00 p.m. Admission charge. Tel: 0203 25555

Exeter   Exeter Maritime Museum, The Quay. The largest collection of working boats on display in the world. The museum is open every day of the year except Christmas Day 10.00 a.m. to 6.00 p.m. from June to September, and 10.00 a.m. to 5.00 p.m. from October to May. Admission charge. Tel: 0392 58075

London   London Transport Museum, Covent Garden, WC2. Open daily 10.00 a.m. to 6.00 p.m. Admission charge. Tel: 071 379 6344

National Maritime Museum, Romney Road, Greenwich, SE10. Open weekdays 10.00 a.m. to 6.00 p.m., Sundays 2.00 p.m. to 5.30 p.m. Admission free. The museum closes at 5.00 p.m. during the winter months. Tel: 071 379 6344

Royal Mews, Buckingham Palace Road, SW1. Open Wednesdays and Thursdays 2.00 p.m. to 4.00 p.m. (except Ascot week). Admission charge.

Stoke Bruerne, nr Towcester   The Waterways Museum. Open daily 10.00 a.m. to 6.00 p.m. from April to September, and 10.00 a.m. to

4.00 p.m. except Mondays from October to March. Admission charge.
Tel: 0604 862229

Swindon   Great Western Railway Museum, Farringdon Road. Open
weekdays 10.00 a.m. to 5.00 p.m., Sundays 2.00 p.m. to 5.00 p.m.
Admission charge. Tel: 0793 26161

Windermere   Steamboat Museum, Rayrigg Road, Bowness-on-
Windermere, Cumbria. Open weekdays Easter to October 10.00 a.m. to
5.00 p.m., Sundays 2.00 p.m. to 5.00 p.m. Admission charge.
Tel: 096 62 5565

York   National Railway Museum, Leeman Road. Open weekdays
10.00 a.m. to 6.00 p.m., Sundays 2.30 p.m. to 6.00 p.m. Admission
charge. Tel: 0904 21261

3.4   EDUCATIONAL TOURS AND EXCHANGES

The Central Bureau for Educational Visits and Exchanges is the UK
Government-funded organisation responsible for all aspects of
information and advice on educational visits and exchanges throughout
the world.
   The Bureau has the following offices:

London   Seymour Mews House, Seymour Mews, London, W1H 9PE.
Tel: 071 486 5101

Edinburgh   3 Bruntsfield Crescent, Edinburgh, EH10 4HD.
Tel: 031 447 8024

Belfast   16 Malone Road, Belfast, BT9 5BN. Tel: 0232 664418/9

Useful information for art and design students

4.1 ART AND DESIGN COURSES

Abbreviations

CNAA	Council for National Academic Awards.
BTEC	Business and Technician Education Council.
UCCA	Universities Central Council on Admissions.
PCAS	Polytechnic Central Admissions System.
ADAR	Art and Design Admissions Registry.

General information

The organisation of post-school education in the United Kingdom is broadly divided, for administrative purposes, into further education, catering for the sixteen to nineteen age range, and higher education for the eighteen-plus age range. There is some considerable overlap between the two groups, and many colleges offer courses covering both further and higher education. The age at entry, academic qualifications, personal preferences and, for art and design applicants, an acceptable folio of work in art and design, normally determines the entry points to the system. It is generally possible to progress from one level to the next and to obtain additional qualifications.

Full-time courses in art and design

Normal minimum age at entry	Course
16	BTEC First Diploma Course (1 year). CPVE (Certificate of pre-vocational education – 1 year). BTEC National Diploma Course (2 years). Foundation Course (2 years).
17	BTEC National Diploma Course with 50 per cent credit for previous experience. Foundation Course (1 year).
18	BTEC Higher National Diploma Course (2 years).

CNAA Diploma of Higher Education Course
(2 years).
CNAA First Degree Course (3 years).
CNAA First Degree (sandwich) Course (4 years).
University First Degree Course (3 years).
Master's Degree Course (1, 2 or 3 years).

Mature students are accepted on most courses subject to their fulfilling
the entry requirements. Many courses are also available for part-time
study.

Course validation and awards

There are two major validating organisations concerned with awards in
art and design in England and Wales. The CNAA validates courses and
makes awards for Degree and Diploma of Higher Education courses.
The Business and Technician Education Council (BTEC), validates
courses and makes awards for National Certificate, National Diploma,
Higher National Certificate and Higher National Diploma courses.
Some universities also validate and make awards for art and design
degree courses such as those at the Slade School and the Courtauld
Institute of Art (University of London). The Royal College of Art is a
postgraduate, university institution.

It is most important that applicants should obtain and study the
prospectuses of the institutions that interest them before making any
application. It is possible to visit some colleges before deciding on a final
choice. Economic and other considerations affect the provision of
education at all levels and may cause changes to be made in the provision
of the courses which are outlined in this chapter. Evidence of creative
potential is given particular emphasis for the majority of courses in art
and design. The possession of the minimum entry qualifications does
not, in itself, entitle an applicant to be admitted to a course.

Degree courses

The majority of degree courses in art and design are validated by the
CNAA and take place in polytechnics. Full-time first degree courses are
usually three years in length or four years if a 'sandwich' element in
industry is included. Sandwich courses include a period spent in a
relevant industry during which the student does not usually receive
financial support from public funds. The normal minimum age for entry
to degree courses is eighteen years. It is possible to study for some
courses by part-time attendance. Entry requirements for degree courses
vary, and it is therefore necessary to refer to the publications of the
CNAA or UCCA who annually publish information and list all the
available courses. The procedures for making an application also vary.
All applications for CNAA art and design degree courses should

normally be made to the Art and Design Admissions Registry (ADAR), Penn House, 9, Broad Street, Hereford, in January of the year of proposed entry to the course. A fee is payable. Students already attending a Foundation or BTEC Diploma or Certificate Course should obtain their application form from their college. Each applicant can list two colleges in order of preference and should also indicate an alternative to the second choice in case the named second-choice college has no vacancies. The processing of the forms is carried out by ADAR, but the individual colleges have the responsibility for all decisions on acceptances. Students who are not successful in obtaining their first, second or alternative choice are notified in June by ADAR of the remaining vacancies that exist. Applicants for university courses should apply to UCCA, PO Box 28, Cheltenham, Gloucestershire GL50 1HY, in the autumn of the year preceding intended entry to the course. A fee is payable. Students in schools and colleges should obtain their UCCA application forms through their tutors. The majority of university first degree courses are in fine art or the history of art, but degree courses are also available which combine other academic disciplines with art and design. The UCCA system enables a choice to be made of not more than five universities/colleges on an application form, naming one course of study at each or specifying alternative courses at the same institution. The processing of all applications is done by UCCA but the individual institution has the responsibility for all decisions on acceptances. If an applicant is not successful in obtaining one of the five choices shown on the form a clearing system is operated by UCCA in the late summer which informs all unplaced candidates of any vacancies that exist. Competition for both CNAA and university degree course places is very heavy. The universities only accept about 35 to 40 per cent of all applicants.

There are a number of degree courses which do not come within the registration schemes of either ADAR or UCCA. The majority of these courses lead to CNAA awards and are available in polytechnics. Information on courses not listed in the publications of ADAR or UCCA can be obtained from the Polytechnic Central Admissions System (PCAS), PO Box 67, Cheltenham, Gloucestershire, GL50 3AP. Full details of the whole range of advanced courses in colleges of further and higher education are given in the *Compendium of Advanced Courses* published annually by the Regional Advisory Councils and obtainable from the London and Home Counties Regional Advisory Council for Technological Education, Tavistock House South, Tavistock Square, London WC1H 9LR. Telephone: 071 388 0027.

Diploma of Higher Education courses

These are two-year full-time or three-year part-time courses leading to a CNAA or university award. They are comparable in standard to the first two years of an Honours degree course and, although regarded as a qualification in their own right, are usually designed to enable students to transfer to a degree course with two years' credit. It is also possible to progress to certain professional qualifications. Entry requirements are similar to those for first degree courses, but intending applicants should obtain full details of the courses that interest them from the colleges concerned. Mature students are particularly catered for on many of these courses. The structure of Diploma of Higher Education courses varies, but generally the courses are of a modular or unit-based programme of study. The minimum age for entry is eighteen years. These courses are not available in Scotland.

Business and Technician Education Council courses
The majority of higher-education courses in art and design other than degree courses are validated by the BTEC. These courses are available at colleges in England and Wales. *Higher National Diploma courses (HND)* normally last for two years of full-time study although a minority of courses may require three years including one year spent in a relevant industry. (Such courses are identified as 'sandwich' courses.) It is also possible to study for some awards on a part-time basis. Applicants for HND courses must be over the age of eighteen years at entry and normally are expected to have previously completed a BTEC National Diploma or a Foundation course to the required standard. The courses are vocational in character and lead directly to employment opportunities. Work experience is normally an integral part of HND courses. These courses are, in general, based on analytical, interpretative and creative design practice, based on a broad development of both practical and organisational skills.

Part-time study at this level can be undertaken by programmes for the *Higher National Certificate*. These course are generally planned over a number of years depending on the needs and experience of the student. They generally cover the specific development of practical skills where creative awareness is developed mainly through the use of processes and materials. All applications for Higher National Diploma courses must be made through ADAR (see pages 114–15).

National Diploma courses (BTEC)
These courses are available at a large number of colleges throughout England and Wales. Applications should be made direct to the college offering the course as early in the expected year of entry as possible. National Diploma courses are either generally broad-based or specific vocational courses or diagnostic courses which demand from the student analytical, interpretative and creative design practice based on a broad understanding of practical skills and related knowledge. The specific vocational courses can lead directly to employment opportunities or a more advanced course such as a degree or HND course. Diagnostic courses are planned to enable students to make an informed choice before applying for a degree or Higher National Diploma course. The minimum age for entry is sixteen years and, for some courses, it is

possible to obtain credit for the first year, in which case the entry age is seventeen years. Specific courses are available in a wide range of disciplines and full details are given on pages 134–44.

National Certificate courses (BTEC)
It is possible to study for BTEC qualifications by part-time attendance at college. Normally such courses form part of an employment package where employers allow attendance at a college for one day per week. The courses are usually unit-based, enabling students to acquire the required number of units for an award over an unspecified period of time.

First Diploma courses (BTEC)
These one-year full-time courses are available at a large number of colleges in England and Wales. They provide a useful introduction to the variety of skills and concepts necessary for a career in design. No formal academic qualifications are required but intending applicants should provide an up-to-date folio of their own creative work when invited to interview. Work experience is normally an integral part of the course. Students can, on successful completion of the course, either take up employment or apply for a place on a National Diploma course.

Continuing Education Units (BTEC)
It is possible to undertake a course or courses of study by part-time attendance at a college which can lead to the award of a BTEC Continuing Education Unit. Courses are designed on a modular basis with each module defined as a Unit. Such courses are planned at all levels and include opportunities for re-training for mature students. Details of such courses can be obtained from the Business and Technician Education Council (BTEC), Central House, Upper Woburn Place, London, WC1 OHH. Tel: 071 636 4100.

Certificate of Pre-Vocational Education (CPVE)
The Joint Board for the Certificate of Pre-Vocational Education (CPVE) validate one-year full-time courses in a number of specialist areas including design. No formal academic entry requirements are needed. Intending applicants for the design areas should provide a folio of recent art and design work when invited for interview. Work experience is an integral part of the course. Successful students can normally apply for places on a BTEC National Diploma course on completion of the CPVE. The majority of local education authorities provide CPVE courses in both schools and colleges.

Foundation courses
These are normally one-year courses of a diagnostic nature, planned, like the BTEC General Art and Design courses, to enable students to experience a wide range of disciplines over a short period of time to

enable them to make an informed choice of a specialism for further study. The majority of these courses are pre-degree, the intention of the students being to progress to a first degree course. The minimum age at entry is usually seventeen years, but there are some two-year courses where the minimum age is sixteen. At the present time Foundation courses are not nationally validated, although many colleges offer an internal validation and external assessment leading to a Regional award. All applications should be made direct to the college offering the course. The academic entry qualifications are normally the same as for a first degree course.

Portfolio requirements for applicants to art and design courses

The majority of colleges offering courses in art and design require applicants to provide, usually at the interview stage, a portfolio of their own work with particular relevance to the course for which application has been made. Information on the recommended contents of the portfolio is usually sent to applicants with the letter inviting the candidate for interview, but some centres make a preliminary assessment based on the contents of a portfolio. The selection and presentation of the work is most important and a suitable folio case is very useful. Cases are available in A1, A2 and A3 sizes from several firms including Daler-Rowney.

Open University Courses

The Open University provides courses leading to the award of a Bachelor of Arts (BA) degree, either with or without honours. Over 130 courses are on offer each year, from faculties and schools of the University and a number of courses will be of interest to art and design students who wish to gain a degree on a part-time basis. No previous academic qualifications are required for entry to the degree programme: the only requirements are that you be over eighteen and resident in the United Kingdom at the start of the academic year.

Courses are either full or half credits: six full credits are required for the award of the BA degree and eight for the award of the degree with honours. All courses last nine months and start in February each year. A full credit requires twelve to fifteen hours a week, whilst a half credit requires the same amount of work over two weeks. Most students gain their degrees after four or five years' study. Study is mainly home-based through specially written correspondence texts, radio and television programmes, and audio and video cassettes, but all students also have a course tutor who may arrange tutorials at local study centres.

The programme of study comprises a foundation course, followed by courses at second, third and fourth level. Courses can be taken from any of the faculties and schools offering courses on the degree programme, although many students 'major' in particular subject areas.

Courses in art and design currently on offer

Arts foundation course (A102)
The Enlightenment (A204)
Culture and belief in Europe 1450–1600 (A205)
Modern art and Modernism: Manet to Pollock (A315)
Liberation and reconstruction: politics, culture and society in
France and Italy 1943–54 (A324)
Art in fifteenth-century Italy (A353)
Arts and society in Britain since the 1930s (A403)

A number of undergraduate courses at second and third levels are
also available for study in the associate student programme. Certificates
of Satisfactory Completion, obtained on successful completion of the
course, can be transferred towards the BA degree at a later date if the
student wishes. Further information on both the degree programme and
the associate student programme can be obtained from: The Central
Enquiry Service, The Open University, PO Box 71, Milton Keynes,
MK7 6AG. Tel: (0908) 653231.

Open College of the Arts

The Open College of the Arts was founded in 1986 with the objective of
providing open learning in the arts. Its methods are in many ways
similar to those of the Open University – particularly in the use of
specially written course books. There is a strong emphasis on tutorial
support, either by regular attendance (on average once a month) at one
of the hundred or so tutorial centres around the United Kingdom or by
exchange of materials with a tutor by post. Tutors are drawn from
practising artists and educators, and tutorial centres range from
universities and colleges to individual artist's studios.

Students are generally expected to work at home for around six
hours a week, and a course lasts for nine months. Course materials
generally comprise the course book(s) and additional textbooks; almost
all of the work is practical activity rather than the writing of essays. One-
year courses available at present include:

Art and Design (an introductory course)
Painting I and II
Sculpture
Textiles
Photography
Creative Writing
Garden Design

There are plans for an art history and a music course. There are no entry
requirements.

Students can if they choose have their work assessed for the OCA
Award at the end of the year, though this is not compulsory. The OCA
Certificate will be presented to students who pursue courses of study
through a number of years, generally at least four. Further details of

courses can be had from: OCA, Houndhill, Worsbrough, Barnsley, S70 6TU.

The Royal College of Art

The College is a postgraduate university institution which awards the degrees of Master of Arts (RCA), Master of Design (RCA), and PhD (RCA). Full-time Master's degree available in the following subjects:

Animation
Architecture
Ceramics and Glass
Computer-Related Design
Conservation (joint course with Victoria and Albert Museum)
Degree by Thesis
Design for Film
Design Management
Fashion Design
Fashion Knitwear
Film Direction
Film Production
Furniture Making
Graphic Design
History of Design (joint course with Victoria and Albert Museum)
Holography
Illustration
Industrial Design
Industrial Design Engineering
Interior Design
Knitted Textiles
Metalwork and Jewellery
Natural History Illustration
Painting
Photography
Printed Textiles
Printmaking
Sculpture
Tapestry
Vehicle Design
Visual Islamic and Traditional Arts
Woven Textiles

The College is organised in four faculties:

Faculty of Design for Communications
Faculty of Design for Manufacture
Faculty of Fine Art
Faculty of Humanities

The majority of students follow courses for two years' duration leading to the Master's degree. Applications should be sent direct to the college.

Vocational part-time courses

Students who wish to study part-time for an examination in a vocational art and design subject, either because they need the qualification or because they wish to undertake the discipline of a structured course, have the choice of a wide range of subjects at all levels. All the major validating and awarding authorities including universities, CNAA and BTEC make awards to students who complete part-time courses. A large number of part-time courses are also available for students who wish to study for the awards of the City and Guilds of London Institute, usually known as City and Guilds. University extra-mural departments, often in association with the Workers Educational Association (WEA), also provide courses. The level of vocational part-time courses varies from those that concentrate on the acquisition of craft skills in areas such as fashion, photography, jewellery, ceramics, furniture and printing to courses at undergraduate and postgraduate level. Fees for these courses are usually less than those for part-time recreational courses, but similar criteria often apply to the minimum numbers required for the initial enrolment. The mode of study also varies from part-time day only to part-time day and evening or part-time evening. Many courses allow for the examinations to be taken in stages to suit the convenience of the students, and courses leading to BTEC awards are often unit based which enables students to acquire individual units over an unspecified period of time.

Recreational part-time courses

A number of colleges organise a wide range of courses during the day and evening for part-time recreational or non-vocational students. The majority of these courses are now self-financing, the cost of the lecturer and the running costs being met from the fee income paid by the students. In order for this system to operate, each course must usually enrol a minimum number of students before it can start, and these initial enrolments can vary according to the nature of the course.

In large urban areas such courses often take place in the local school or college of art and design or in colleges of further education. Sometimes evening courses are held in the art departments of local secondary schools. In rural areas courses may be held in village halls, junior schools or similar accommodation. Enrolment usually takes place once a year, in September, and courses usually meet once a week for three terms. The number of meetings can, however, vary from about thirty-six at the maximum to short courses of six, eight or ten meetings. Students normally have to provide all their own materials, and for some specialised activities such as pottery or jewellery payment of a studio fee is sometimes required. Information on the availability of courses is usually published in the local press, and details can often be obtained from local public libraries as well as from the local colleges.

Degree courses: CNAA

Multidisciplinary courses including multi-media

The following courses embrace more than one field in art and design and are, therefore, listed separately from courses in specific areas of study. In this section FT = full-time, PT = part-time, HE = higher education. The addresses of all colleges listed in this handbook are shown in Section 4.6.

Bradford and Ilkley Community College: BA, FT – 3 years. Art and Design. Students choose to study two areas from the following: two-dimensional design, textile media, three-dimensional design and also from fine arts, community arts and design.

Cambridgeshire College of Arts and Technology: BA Honours, FT – 3 years, PT and/or mixed mode – 4/6 years. Humanities/Social Studies.

Crewe and Alsager College of Higher Education: BA, FT – 3 years. Combined Studies (Crafts): subjects include ceramics, graphic design, print-making and typography, jewellery, photography, textiles and wood.

Dartington College of Arts: Dip. HE, FT – 2 years. Art and Social Context (the relationship of art and artist to the broader community).

Duncan of Jordanstone College of Art: BA/BA Honours, FT – 4 years. Design: ceramics, graphic design, illustration, interior design, jewellery and silversmithing, printed textiles, product design and woven textiles.

BA/BA Honours, FT – 4 years. Fine Art (Painting and Sculpture): the course includes both fine art and design elements. In years 2, 3 and 4 students specialise in drawing and painting or sculpture.

Exeter Faculty of Art and Design (Polytechnic of the South West): BA (Honours) Design, FT – 3 years. Specialisms in Graphic Design/Three-dimensional Design.

Glasgow School of Art: BA/BA Honours, FT – 4 years. Art: the first year of the course includes both fine art and design elements. In years 2, 3 and 4 students may specialise in painting, print-making, sculpture, murals or stained glass, or may pursue studies in all of these. A complementary design subject may be studied by arrangement.

BA/BA Honours, FT – 4 years. Design: the first year includes both fine art and design elements, after which students specialise in one of the following: ceramics, embroidered and woven textiles, furniture/interior/product design, graphic design, printed textiles or silversmithing and jewellery. Complementary studies in design or fine art may be arranged.

London College of Printing (London Institute): BA Honours (sandwich) – 4 years. Media and Production Design: studies include photography, visual research and analysis, typography and letter design, printing processes and techniques. In the second year and beyond, options are publicity design, information design and communication media design.

Maidstone College of Art and Design (Kent Institute): BA Honours, FT – 3 years. Communication Media.

Manchester Polytechnic: BA Honours, FT – 3 years. Design for Communication.

Newcastle-upon-Tyne Polytechnic: BA Honours, FT – 3 years. Media Production.

North Staffordshire Polytechnic: BA Honours, FT – 3 years. Design: major study specialisms are typographic design, audio-visual design, illustration, photography, domestic products, industrial tableware and holloware, printed surface pattern, designer/craftsman ceramics, architectural and sculptural ceramics and designer/craftsman glass.

Robert Gordon's Institute of Technology: BA/BA Honours, FT – 4 years. Design and Craft: in the first year students take a range of subjects which include design and crafts, drawing and painting, sculpture and print-making. In year 2 fine art subjects are discontinued. In years 3 and 4 students select two subjects from ceramics, graphic design, jewellery, printed textiles and woven textiles with the option of dropping one in the fourth year. Woven Textiles is approved as a main study subject at degree level only.

BA/BA Honours, FT – 4 years. Fine Art: in the first year students take a range of subjects which include design and crafts, drawing and painting, sculpture and print-making. In year 2 design and crafts are discontinued. In years 3 and 4 drawing and painting or sculpture is studied with an option of a supporting subject.

Fine art

A fine art course may be based on the traditional activities of painting, sculpture, drawing and print-making, or it may encourage the students to use other media or combinations of media. In either case, a course in this area is likely to be relatively open-ended, taking its direction from the creative development of the individual student. All courses contain elements of critical and theoretical studies, including the history of art and design.

Bath College of Higher Education (incorporating Bath Academy of Art): BA Honours, FT – 3 years.

Birmingham Institute of Art and Design (City of Birmingham Polytechnic): BA Honours, FT – 3 years.

Brighton Polytechnic: BA Honours, FT – 3 years.

Bristol Polytechnic: BA Honours, FT – 3 years.

Camberwell School of Art and Crafts (London Institute): BA Honours, FT – 3 years.

Canterbury College of Art and Design (Kent Institute): BA Honours, FT – 3 years.

Central School of Art and Design (London Institute): BA Honours, FT – 3 years.
Chelsea School of Art (London Institute): BA Honours, FT – 3 years.
Coventry (Lanchester) Polytechnic: BA Honours, FT – 3 years.
Duncan of Jordanstone College of Art: BA/BA Honours, FT – 4 years.
Exeter Faculty of Art and Design (Plymouth Polytechnic): BA Honours, FT – 3 years.
Falmouth School of Art and Design: BA Honours, FT – 3 years.
Glasgow School of Art: BA/BA Honours, FT – 4 years. Art.
Gloucestershire College of Arts and Technology: BA Honours, FT – 3 years.
Goldsmith's College: BA Honours, FT – 3 years.
Gwent College of Higher Education: BA Honours, FT – 3 years.
Humberside College of Higher Education: BA Honours, FT – 3 years.
Kingston Polytechnic: BA Honours, FT – 3 years.
Lancashire Polytechnic: BA Honours, FT – 3 years.
Leeds Polytechnic: BA Honours, FT – 3 years.
Leicester Polytechnic: BA Honours, FT – 3 years.
Liverpool Polytechnic: BA Honours, FT – 3 years.
Loughborough College of Art and Design: BA Honours, FT – 3 years.
Manchester Polytechnic: BA Honours, FT – 3 years.
Middlesex Polytechnic: BA Honours, FT – 3 years.
Newcastle-upon-Tyne Polytechnic: BA Honours, FT – 3 years.
Norfolk College of Art and Design: BA Honours, FT – 3 years.
North-East London Polytechnic: BA Honours, FT – 3 years.
North Staffordshire Polytechnic: BA Honours, FT – 3 years.
Robert Gordon's Institute of Technology: BA/BA Honours, FT – 4 years.
St Martin's School of Art (London Institute): BA Honours, FT – 3 years.
Sheffield City Polytechnic: BA Honours, FT – 3 years.
South Glamorgan Institute of Higher Education: BA Honours, FT – 3 years.
Stourbridge College of Technology and Art: BA Honours, FT – 3 years.
Sunderland Polytechnic: BA Honours, FT – 3 years.
Trent Polytechnic: BA Honours, FT – 3 years.
Ulster University: BA Honours, FT – 3 years.
West Surrey College of Art and Design: BA Honours, FT – 3 years.
Wimbledon School of Art: BA Honours, FT – 3 years.
Winchester School of Art: BA Honours, FT – 3 years.
Wolverhampton Polytechnic: BA Honours, FT – 3 years.

Graphic design

Graphic design courses are mainly concerned with visual communication, particularly the techniques and disciplines that have to do with design for print, e.g. typography, graphic reproduction and illustration. To these, many add an introduction (and some add more than an introduction) to film and television graphics. Some courses place an emphasis on subjective illustration, some on information graphics, some on publicity and advertising. All courses contain an element of complementary studies, including the history of art and design. Some related courses are listed in the section on Art and design multidisciplinary courses.

Bath College of Higher Education (incorporating Bath Academy of Art): BA Honours, FT – 3 years.

Birmingham Institute of Art and Design (City of Birmingham Polytechnic): BA Honours, FT – 3 years.

Brighton Polytechnic: BA Honours, FT – 3 years.

Bristol Polytechnic: BA Honours, FT – 3 years.

Camberwell School of Art and Crafts (London Institute): BA Honours, FT – 3 years.

Chelsea School of Art (London Institute): BA Honours, FT – 3 years.

Coventry (Lanchester) Polytechnic: BA Honours, FT – 3 years.

Duncan of Jordanstone College of Art: BA/BA Honours, FT – 4 years, Design.

Falmouth School of Art and Design: BA Honours, FT – 3 years. BA Honours (sandwich) – 4 years.

Glasgow School of Art: BA/BA Honours, FT – 4 years. Design.

Gwent College of Higher Education: BA Honours, FT – 3 years.

Harrow College of Higher Education: BA Honours, FT – 3 years. Graphic Information Design.

Humberside College of Higher Education: BA Honours, FT – 3 years.

Kingston Polytechnic: BA Honours, FT – 3 years.

Lancashire Polytechnic: BA Honours (sandwich) – 4 years.

Leeds Polytechnic: BA Honours, FT – 3 years.

Leicester Polytechnic: BA Honours, FT – 3 years.

Liverpool Polytechnic: BA Honours, FT – 3 years.

London College of Printing (London Institute): BA Honours, FT – 3 years.

Maidstone College of Art (Kent Institute): BA Honours, FT – 3 years.

Middlesex Polytechnic: BA Honours, FT – 3 years. BA Honours (sandwich) – 4 years. Scientific and Technical Illustration.

Newcastle-upon-Tyne Polytechnic: BA Honours, FT – 3 years.

Norfolk College of Art and Design: BA Honours FT – 3 years.

North Staffordshire Polytechnic: BA Honours, FT – 3 years. Design.

Ravensbourne College of Design and Communication: BA Honours, FT – 3 years.

Robert Gordon's Institute of Technology: BA/BA Honours, FT – 4 years. Design and Craft.

St Martin's School of Art (London Institute): BA Honours, FT – 3 years.

Trent Polytechnic: BA Honours, FT – 3 years. Information Graphics.

Ulster University: BA Honours, FT – 3 years.

Wolverhampton Polytechnic: BA Honours, FT – 3 years.

History of art and design

These courses concentrate mainly on the modern period. The opportunity to engage in some practical studio work occurs, the aim of which is to support the historical studies and deepen the student's understanding of the work of the artist and the designer. There are no special entry requirements for these courses, and applications should be addressed direct to the polytechnic offering the course and not through the Art and Design Admissions Registry. History of art and design also appears as an option in certain Arts and Humanities and Multidisciplinary courses. For further information on such courses consult the *CNAA Directory* (see Bibliography, p. 158).

Brighton Polytechnic: BA Honours, FT – 3 years. History of Design.

Camberwell School of Arts and Crafts (London Institute): BA Honours, FT – 3 years. History of Drawing and Printmaking.

Leicester Polytechnic: BA/BA Honours, FT – 3 years. History of Art and Design in the Modern Period.

Manchester Polytechnic: BA Honours, FT – 3 years. History of Design.

Middlesex Polytechnic: BA Honours, FT – 3 years. History of Art, Design and Film.

Newcastle-upon-Tyne Polytechnic: BA/BA Honours, FT – 3 years, PT – 5 years. History of Modern Art, Design and Film.

North Staffordshire Polytechnic: BA Honours, FT – 3 years. History of Design and the Visual Arts.

Sheffield City Polytechnic: BA Honours, FT – 3 years. History of Art, Design and Film.

Photography, film and video

These courses are specialist first degree courses. Some Fine Art and Graphic Design courses also contain studies in photography and film/video. Entry requirements for these courses vary and applicants are advised to obtain the institutions' prospectuses for details.

Central London Polytechnic: BA Honours, FT – 3 years, Film, Video and Photographic Arts: subjects include visual studies, aesthetics and communication studies.

BSc/BSc Honours, FT – 3 years. Photographic Sciences: the course provides two options – photographic technology and scientific photography – and is designed for those wishing to work on the scientific side of the photographic industry or as scientific photographers in industry or government.

Derbyshire College of Higher Education, Derby: BA Honours, FT – 3 years. Photographic Studies: the course is a practical visual arts course with photography and allied subjects as the principal means of expression.

Harrow College of Higher Education: BA Honours, FT – 3 years. Applied Photography, Film and Television: students study technical theory and also aesthetics and sociology which are used to develop awareness of the value and place of photography, film and television in comparison with other media. Options include cultural and commercial applications of photography and scientific and industrial applications of photography, film and television.

BA, PT – 2 years. Photographic Media Studies: the course is designed to allow holders of the Professional Qualifying Examination of the Institute of Incorporated Photographers (IIPPQE) to read for a degree.

London College of Printing (London Institute): BA Honours, FT – 3 years. Visual Communication, Photography, Film and Video. The course provides a broad education in visual communication, developing theoretical, technical and professional skills and knowledge. Specialisation in either photography or film and video is possible in the later stages.

Trent Polytechnic: BA Honours, FT – 3 years. Photography: the course is concerned with the study and exploration of the fundamental nature of photography, of how equipment and materials currently available determine its potential and how conventions of quality and previous usage affect the understanding of photographs.

West Surrey College of Art and Design: BA Honours, FT – 3 years. Photography, Film and Video, Animation.

Textiles/fashion

In the area of textiles fashion, colleges are approved to conduct courses in 'chief studies' and supporting studies, e.g. fashion, embroidery, woven and printed textiles. As in other art and design courses, courses in textiles/fashion contain an element of complementary studies, including the history of art and design. Visits to fashion and textile centres abroad are encouraged; for students whose chief study is fashion, they are obligatory.

Birmingham Institute of Art and Design (City of Birmingham Polytechnic): BA Honours, FT – 3 years. Chief studies: embroidery, fashion, woven and printed textiles.

Bretton Hall College, Wakefield: BA Honours, FT – 3 years. Textile Arts.

Brighton Polytechnic: BA Honours (sandwich) – 4 years. Fashion, Textiles Design and Administration.

Bristol Polytechnic: BA Honours, FT – 3 years. Chief study: fashion.

Central School of Art and Design (London Institute): BA Honours, FT – 3 years. Chief study: woven and printed textiles.

Duncan of Jordanstone College of Art: BA/BA Honours, FT – 4 years. Design (see also multidisciplinary courses).

Glasgow School of Art: BA/BA Honours, FT – 4 years. Design (see also multidisciplinary courses).

Gloucestershire College of Arts and Technology: BA Honours, FT – 3 years. Chief study: fashion.

Goldsmiths' College: BA Honours, FT – 3 years. Chief study: embroidery.

Harrow College of Higher Education: BA Honours, FT – 3 years. Chief study: fashion.

Huddersfield Polytechnic: BSc Honours (sandwich) – 4 years. Textile Design.

Kidderminster College of Further Education: BA Honours (sandwich) – 4 years. Design of Carpets and Related Textiles.

Kingston Polytechnic: BA Honours, FT – 3 years. Chief study: fashion.

Lancashire Polytechnic: BA Honours, FT – 3 years.
BA Honours (sandwich) – 4 years.

Leicester Polytechnic: BA Honours, FT – 3 years. Chief studies: fashion, woven and printed textiles, contour fashion, footwear design.

Liverpool Polytechnic: BA Honours, FT – 3 years. Chief studies: fashion, woven and printed textiles.

Loughborough College of Art and Design: BA Honours, FT – 3 years. Chief studies: embroidery, woven and printed textiles.

Manchester Polytechnic: BA Honours, FT – 3 years. Chief studies: fashion, embroidery, woven and printed textiles.

Middlesex Polytechnic: BA Honours, FT – 3 years. Chief studies: fashion, woven and printed textiles.

Newcastle-upon-Tyne Polytechnic: BA Honours (sandwich) – 4 years. Fashion.

North East London Polytechnic: BA Honours (sandwich) – 4 years. Fashion with Marketing.

Ravensbourne College of Art and Design: BA Honours, FT – 3 years. Chief study: fashion.

Robert Gordon's Institute of Technology: BA/BA Honours, FT – 4 years. Design and Craft (see also multidisciplinary courses).

St Martin's School of Art (London Institute): BA Honours, FT – 3 years. Chief study: fashion.
BA Honours (sandwich) – 4 years. Fashion.

Scottish College of Textiles: BA Honours, FT – 4 years. Industrial Design (Textiles).

Trent Polytechnic: BA Honours, FT – 3 years. Chief studies: fashion, textile design.
BA Honours (sandwich) – 4 years. Knitwear Design.

Ulster University: BA Honours, FT – 3 years. Chief studies: embroidery, woven and printed textiles.

West Surrey College of Art and Design: BA Honours, FT – 3 years. Chief study: woven and printed textiles.

Winchester School of Art: BA Honours, FT – 3 years. Chief study: woven and printed textiles.

Three-dimensional design

In the area of three-dimensional design, colleges are approved to conduct courses in 'chief studies'. Examples of chief studies are furniture design, ceramics and interior design. In some cases, a course has been approved which is an amalgam; wood/metal/ceramics/plastics, for example. Where colleges offer courses in more than one chief study in the three-dimensional design area, some treat them as quite separate courses, while some offer a course which begins as a general course and divides at some point to focus on particular chief studies. All courses in this area contain a supporting study or studies and complementary studies, including the history of art and design.

Bath College of Higher Education (incorporating Bath Academy of Art): BA Honours, FT – 3 years. Chief study: ceramics.

Birmingham Institute of Art and Design (City of Birmingham Polytechnic): BA Honours, FT – 3 years. Chief studies: ceramics with glass, furniture, industrial design (engineering), interior design, jewellery and silversmithing, theatre design.

Brighton Polytechnic: BA Honours, FT – 3 years. Chief studies: interior design, wood/metal/ceramics/plastics.

Bristol Polytechnic: BA Honours, FT – 3 years. Chief studies: ceramics, wood, metal and plastics.

Buckinghamshire College of Higher Education: BA Honours, FT – 3 years. Chief studies: ceramics with glass, furniture, interior design, silver/metal.

Camberwell School of Art and Crafts (London Institute): BA Honours, FT – 3 years. Chief studies: ceramics, silver/metal.

Central School of Art and Design (London Institute): BA Honours, FT – 3 years. Chief studies: ceramics, industrial design (engineering), jewellery, theatre design.

City of London Polytechnic: BA Honours (sandwich) – 4 years. Silversmithing, Jewellery and Allied Crafts.

Coventry (Lanchester) Polytechnic: BA Honours (sandwich) – 4 years. Industrial Design Transportation.

Duncan of Jordanstone College of Art: BA/BA Honours, FT – 4 years. Design (see also multidisciplinary courses).

Glasgow School of Art: BA/BA Honours, FT – 4 years. Design (see also multidisciplinary courses).

Gwent College of Higher Education: BA Honours, FT – 3 years.

Kingston Polytechnic: BA Honours, FT – 3 years. Chief studies: furniture, interior design.

Leeds Polytechnic: BA Honours, FT – 3 years. Chief studies: furniture, industrial design (engineering), interior design.

Leicester Polytechnic: BA Honours, FT – 3 years. Chief studies: ceramics, furniture, industrial design (engineering), interior design, silversmithing.

Liverpool Institute of Higher Education: B.Des. Honours, FT – 3 years. Art with Design and Technology.

Loughborough College of Art and Design: BA Honours, FT – 3 years. Chief studies: ceramics, furniture, silversmithing and jewellery.

Manchester Polytechnic: BA Honours, FT – 3 years. Chief studies: industrial design (engineering), interior design, wood/metal/ceramics.

Middlesex Polytechnic: BA Honours, FT – 3 years. Chief studies: ceramics, furniture, silver/metal.
BA Honours (sandwich – 4 years. Interior design.
BA Honours (sandwich) – 4 years. Jewellery and Ceramics.

Napier College: BSc (sandwich) – 4 years. Industrial Design (Technology).

Newcastle-upon-Tyne Polytechnic: BA Honours, FT – 3 years. Design Craftsmanship.
  BA Honours (sandwich) – 4 years. Design for Industry, Wood, Metal and Plastics.

North London Polytechnic: BA, FT – 3 years. Interior Design.

Ravensbourne College of Design and Communications, Chislehurst: BA Honours, FT – 3 years. Product Design.

Robert Gordon's Institute of Technology: BA/BA Honours, FT – 4 years. Design and Craft (see also multidisciplinary courses).

Sheffield City Polytechnic: BA Honours, FT – 3 years. Chief studies: industrial design (engineering), silversmithing and jewellery.

South Glamorgan Institute of Higher Education: BA Honours, FT – 3 years. Chief studies: ceramics, industrial design.

Stourbridge College of Technology and Art: BA Honours, FT – 3 years. Chief study: glass.

Sunderland Polytechnic: BA Honours, FT – 3 years. Chief study: glass with ceramics.

Teeside Polytechnic: BA Honours, FT – 3 years. Chief studies: industrial design (engineering), interior design.

Trent Polytechnic: BA Honours, FT – 3 years. Theatre Design.
  BA Honours (sandwich) – 4 years. Furniture Design.
  BA Honours (sandwich) – 4 years. Interior Design.
  BA Honours (sandwich) – 4 years. Knitwear Design.

Ulster Polytechnic: BA Honours, FT – 3 years. Chief studies: ceramics, furniture, interior design, silversmithing and jewellery.

West Surrey College of Art and Design: BA Honours, FT – 3 years. Chief studies: ceramics, glass, metals.

Wimbledon School of Art: BA Honours, FT – 3 years. Chief study: theatre design.

Wolverhampton Polytechnic: BA Honours, FT – 3 years. Chief studies: ceramics, wood/metal/plastics.

BTEC courses

The BTEC validated courses listed may be subject to alteration or amendment. Full information on the availability of all BTEC courses may be obtained from: Business and Technician Education Council (BTEC), Central House, Upper Woburn Place, London, WC1H 0HH. Tel: 071 388 3288 or from the colleges. The courses are shown under broad subject groupings and the full title of the course may vary from that given in this handbook.

Higher National Diploma courses: BTEC

The following courses generally require two years of full-time study from the minimum age of entry of eighteen years.

Architectural stained glass
West Glamorgan Institute of Higher Education, Swansea. FT – 2 years.

Ceramics including studio pottery
Croydon College. FT – 2 years.
Falmouth School of Art and Design. FT – 2 years.
Harrow College of Higher Education. FT – 2 years.
North Staffordshire Polytechnic. FT – 2 years.
West Glamorgan Institute of Higher Education, Swansea. FT – 2 years.

Conservation and Restoration Studies
Lincolnshire College of Art and Design, Lincoln. FT – 2 years.

Design (communications)
Cleveland College of Art and Design. FT – 2 years.
Dewsbury College. FT – 2 years.
Gloucestershire College of Arts and Technology, Gloucester, (Electronic
   Media). FT – 2 years.
North-East Wales Institute of Higher Education, Wrexham. FT – 2 years.
Northbrook College of Design and Technology, Worthing, (Audio-Visual).
   FT – 2 years.
Northumberland College of Arts and Technology, Ashington. FT – 2 years.
Norton College Sheffield/Sheffield Polytechnic. FT – 2 years.
Suffolk College of Higher and Further Education, Ipswich. FT – 2 years.
Wolverhampton Polytechnic. FT – 2 years.

Design Crafts
City of Birmingham Polytechnic. FT – 2 years.
Carmarthenshire College of Technology and Art, Llanelli. FT – 2 years.
Chelsea School of Art (London Institute). FT – 2 years.
Cumbria College of Art and Design, Carlisle. FT – 2 years.
Derbyshire College of Higher Education, Derby. FT – 2 years.
Epsom School of Art and Design. FT – 2 years.
Medway College of Design (Kent Institute), Rochester. FT – 2 years.
North-East Wales Institute of Higher Education, Wrexham. FT – 2 years.

Design (Film/Television)
Bournemouth and Poole College of Art and Design, Poole. FT – 2 years.
Gwent College of Higher Education, Newport. FT – 2 years.
Ravensbourne College of Design and Communication, Chislehurst
   (Television Programme Operations). FT – 2 years.

Design (Illustration)
Blackpool and Fylde College. FT – 2 years.
Cambridgeshire College of Arts and Technology, Cambridge. FT – 2 years.

Design (Modelmaking)
Hertfordshire College of Art and Design. FT – 2 years.
Medway College of Design (Kent Institute), Rochester. FT – 2 years.

Design (Multi-Disciplinary)
Portsmouth College of Art, Design and Further Education. FT – 2 years.
Stockport College of Technology. FT – 2 years.

Fashion (including fashion/textile design)
Berkshire College of Art and Design, Maidenhead. FT – 2 years.
Bournemouth and Poole College of Art and Design, Poole. FT – 2 years.
Central School of Speech and Drama, London. FT – 2 years.
Cleveland College of Art and Design, Middlesbrough. FT – 2 years.
Derbyshire College of Higher Education, Derby. FT – 2 years.
Dewsbury College. FT – 2 years.
Epsom School of Art and Design. FT – 2 years.
London College of Fashion (London Institute). FT – 2 years.
Medway College of Design (Kent Institute), Rochester. FT – 2 years.
Northbrook College of Design and Technology, Worthing. FT – 2 years.
Salford College of Technology. FT – 2 years.
Southampton Institute of Higher Education. FT – 2 years.
York College of Arts and Technology (Stage Management). FT – 2 years.

Graphic Design
Amersham College of Further Education Art and Design. FT – 2 years.
Barnet College/Middlesex Polytechnic. FT – 2 years.
Berkshire College of Art and Design, Maidenhead. FT – 2 years.
Blackpool and Fylde College of Further and Higher Education. FT – 2 years.
Bolton Institute of Higher Education. FT – 2 years.
Bournemouth and Poole College of Art and Design, Poole. FT – 2 years.
Colchester Institute. FT – 2 years.
Croydon College. FT – 2 years.
Cumbria College of Art and Design, Carlisle. FT – 2 years.
Derbyshire College of Higher Education, Derby. FT – 2 years.
Doncaster Metropolitan Institute of Higher Education. FT – 2 years.
Dunstable College. FT – 2 years.
Epsom School of Art and Design. FT – 2 years.
Falmouth School of Art and Design. FT – 2 years.
Hounslow Borough College. FT – 2 years.
Lincolnshire College of Art and Design, Lincoln. FT – 2 years.
London College of Printing (London Institute). FT – 2 years.
Loughborough College of Art and Design. FT – 2 years.
Medway College of Art and Design (Kent Institute), Rochester. FT – 2 years.
Nene College, Northampton. FT – 2 years.
Newcastle-upon-Tyne College of Arts and Technology. FT – 2 years.

Newham Community College, London. FT – years.
Norfolk College of Art and Design, Norwich. FT – 2 years.
Plymouth College of Art and Design. FT – 2 years.
Richmond upon Thames College. FT – 2 years.
Salford College of Technology. FT – 2 years.
Salisbury College of Art. FT – 2 years.
Somerset College of Arts and Technology. FT – 2 years.
Southampton Institute of Higher Education. FT – 2 years.
South Glamorgan Institute of Higher Education, Cardiff. FT – 2 years.
Stourbridge College of Technology and Art. FT – 2 years.
Swindon College. FT – 2 years.
Watford College. FT – 2 years.
York College of Arts and Technology. FT – 2 years.

Paper Conservation/Book Restoration
Camberwell School of Arts and Crafts (London Institute). FT – 2 years.
   (Paper/book.)

Photography
Blackpool and Fylde College of Further and Higher Education. FT – 2 years.
Bournemouth and Poole College of Art and Design, Poole. FT – 2 years.
Gloucestershire College of Arts and Technology, Gloucester. FT – 2 years.
Gwent College of Higher Education, Newport. FT – 2 years.
Manchester Polytechnic. FT – 2 years.
Medway College of Art and Design (Kent Institute), Rochester. FT – 2 years.
Newcastle-upon-Tyne College of Arts and Technology. FT – 2 years.
Plymouth College of Art and Design. FT – 2 years.
Salisbury College of Art. FT – 2 years.
West Glamorgan Institute of Higher Education, Swansea. FT – 2 years.

Spatial Design including exhibition/interior design
Bournemouth and Poole College of Art and Design, Poole. FT – 2 years.
College for the Distributive Trades (London Institute). FT – 2 years.
Dewsbury College. FT – 2 years.
Humberside College of Higher Education, Hull. FT – 2 years.
London College of Furniture (City of London Polytechnic). FT – 2 years.
Medway College of Art and Design (Kent Institute), Rochester. FT – 2 years.
Newcastle-upon-Tyne College of Arts and Technology. FT – 2 years.
Salford College of Technology. FT – 2 years.

Technical Illustration
Birmingham Institute of Art and Design (City of Birmingham Polytechnic). FT – 2 years.

Bournemouth and Poole College of Art and Design, Poole. FT – 2 years.
Falmouth School of Art and Design. FT – 2 years.
Portsmouth College of Art, Design and Further Education. FT – 2 years.
Sunderland Polytechnic. FT – 2 years.
West Glamorgan Institute of Higher Education, Swansea. FT – 2 years.

Textile Design
Blackburn College of Technology and Design. FT – 2 years.
Chelsea School of Art (London Institute). FT – 2 years.
Cleveland College of Art and Design. FT – 2 years.
Derbyshire College of Higher Education, Derby. FT – 2 years.
Huddersfield Polytechnic. FT – 2 years.
Somerset College of Arts and Technology, Taunton. FT – 2 years.

Theatre Studies
Croydon College. FT – 2 years.
London College of Fashion (London Institute). FT – 2 years.
Liverpool City College. FT – 2 years.

Three-Dimensional Studies
Berkshire College of Art and Design, Maidenhead. FT – 2 years.
  (Exhibition/Industrial/Interior.)
Bournemouth and Poole College of Art and Design, Poole. FT – 2 years.
  (Industrial.)
Chelsea School of Art (London Institute). FT – 2 years. (Interior/Product
  Design.)
Colchester Institute. FT – 2 years.
Epsom School of Art and Design. FT – 2 years.
Huddersfield Polytechnic. Sandwich Course – 3 years. (Product Design.)
Lancashire Polytechnic, Preston. FT – 2 years. (Wood/Metal/Ceramics.)
Sheffield City Polytechnic/Norton College. FT – 2 years. (Product
  Packaging.)
Southampton Institute of Higher Education. FT – 2 years. (Industrial
  Design/Maritime.)
Suffolk College of Higher and Further Education, Ipswich. FT – 2 years.
  (Exhibition/Scenic.)
Swindon College. FT – 2 years. (Packaging.)

BTEC National Diploma Courses
The following courses generally require two years of full-time study
from the minimum age of entry of sixteen years.

Audio Visual/Film/TV
Brunel Technical College, Bristol.
Central Manchester College.
Dewsbury College.
Epsom School of Art and Design.

Harrogate College of Arts and Technology.
Havering Technical College, Hornchurch.
Kidderminster College of Further Education.
Longlands College of Further Education, Middlesbrough.
Lowestoft College.
Northbrook College of Design and Technology, Worthing.
North-East Wales Institute of Higher Education, Wrexham.
North Warwickshire College of Technology and Art, Nuneaton.
Portsmouth College of Art, Design and Further Education.
Sandwell College of Further and Higher Education, Wednesbury.
South Nottinghamshire College of Further Education, West Bridgeford.
South Thames College.
Southend College of Technology.

Ceramics
Harrogate College of Arts and Technology.
Lowestoft College.
North Warwickshire College of Technology and Art, Nuneaton.
Plymouth College of Art and Design.
Rotherham College of Arts and Technology.
Royal Forest of Dean College, Cinderford.
York College of Arts and Technology.

Clothing
Belfast College of Technology.
Central Manchester College.
Colchester Institute.
Dacorum College, Hemel Hempstead.
Erith College of Technology, Belvedere.
Handsworth Technical College, Birmingham.
Hinkley College of Further Education.
Jacob Kramer College, Leeds.
Kilburn Polytechnic.
Liverpool City College.
London College of Fashion (London Institute).
Montgomery College of Further Education, Newtown.
Oxford College of Further Education.
Southgate Technical College, London.

Conservation Crafts
Lincolnshire College of Art and Design, Lincoln.
Camberwell School of Arts and Crafts (London Institute).

Creative Software
Norton College, Sheffield.

Exhibition/Display/Interior Design
Note: Not all colleges offer all three options.
Bournemouth and Poole College of Art and Design, Poole.
Bournville College of Art (Birmingham Institute of Art and Design).
Bradfield and Ilkley Community College.
Cassio College, Watford.
College for the Distributive Trades (London Institute).
Dewsbury College.
Harrogate College of Arts and Technology.
Hastings College of Arts and Technology, St Leonards-on-Sea.
Herefordshire College of Art and Design, Hereford.
Hounslow Borough College.
Humberside College of Higher Education, Hull.
Isle College, Wisbech.
Jacob Kramer College, Leeds.
Liverpool City College.
London College of Furniture (City of London Polytechnic).
Medway College of Art and Design (Kent Institute), Rochester.
Mid-Cheshire College of Further Education, Northwich.
Parkwood College, Sheffield.
Plymouth College of Art and Design.
Portsmouth College of Art, Design and Further Education.
South Devon College of Arts and Technology, Torquay.
Southend College of Technology.
Southgate Technical College.
Tameside College of Technology, Ashton-under-Lyme.
Trowbridge College.
Uxbridge Technical College.
Ware College.
Willesden College of Technology.
Windsor and Maidenhead College of Further Education.
Wirral Metropolitan College, Wallasey.

Fashion Design
Barnet College.
Barnfield College, Luton.
Berkshire College of Art, Maidenhead.
Boston College of Further Education.
Bournemouth and Poole College of Art and Design, Poole.
Bradford and Ilkley Community College.
Cauldon College of Further and Higher Education, Stoke-on-Trent.
Central Manchester College.
Chesterfield College of Technology and Arts.
Cleveland College of Art and Design, Middlesbrough.
Coventry Technical College.
Croydon College.
Derbyshire College of Higher Education, Derby.

Dewsbury College.
Doncaster Metropolitan Institute of Higher Education.
East Warwickshire College of Further Education, Rugby.
Epsom School of Art and Design.
Gloucestershire College of Arts and Technology.
Gwent College of Higher Education, Newport.
Hastings College of Arts and Technology, St Leonards-on-Sea.
Hounslow Borough College.
Isle College, Wisbech.
Jacob Kramer College, Leeds.
Lincolnshire College of Art and Design.
London College of Fashion (London Institute).
Loughborough College of Art and Design.
Medway College of Art and Design (Kent Institute), Rochester.
Nene College, Northampton.
Newcastle-upon-Tyne College of Arts and Technology.
North Warwickshire College of Technology and Art, Nuneaton.
Northbrook College of Design and Technology, Worthing.
Norfolk College of Art and Design, Norwich.
Parkwood Tertiary College, Sheffield.
Plymouth College of Art and Design.
Salford College of Technology.
Salisbury College of Art.
Somerset College of Arts and Technology, Taunton.
Southampton Institute of Higher Education.
South Fields College of Further Education, Leicester.
Stafford College of Further Education.
Tameside College of Technology, Ashton-under-Lyme.
West Nottinghamshire College of Further Education, Mansfield.
Wigan College of Technology.

Fashion and Textile Design
Canterbury College of Art and Design (Kent Institute).
Northbrook College of Design and Technology, Worthing.
Rotherham College of Arts and Technology.
Southend College of Technology.
Southport College of Art and Technology.
York College of Arts and Technology.

Footwear Design
Cordwainers Technical College, London.
Nene College, Northampton.
Stafford College of Further Education.

Furniture Design
Jacob Kramer College, Leeds.
London College of Furniture (City of London Polytechnic).

General Art and Design
Accrington and Rossendale College.
Amersham College of Further Education, Art and Design.
Barnet College.
Barnfield College, Luton.
Barnsley College of Art and Design.
Basingstoke Technical College.
Bedford College of Higher Education.
Blackburn College of Technology and Design.
Bournemouth and Poole College of Art and Design, Poole.
Bournville College of Art (Birmingham Institute of Art and Design).
Burnley College of Technology.
Chelsea School of Art (London Institute).
Chester College of Further Education.
Chesterfield College of Technology and Arts.
City and East London College.
Cleveland College of Art and Design, Middlesbrough.
Coventry Technical College.
Crosskeys College.
Croydon College.
Derbyshire College of Higher Education.
East Surrey College.
East Warwickshire College of Further Education.
Eastbourne College of Arts and Technology.
Epsom School of Art and Design.
Exeter Faculty of Art and Design.
Falmouth School of Art and Design.
Gwynedd Technical College.
Halton College of Further Education.
Harlow College.
Harrogate College of Arts and Technology.
Havering Technical College.
Herefordshire College of Art and Design, Hereford.
Hounslow Borough College.
Huddersfield Technical College.
Isle College, Wisbech.
Kingsway-Princeton College, London.
Lancaster and Morecambe College of Further Education.
Leigh College, Greater Manchester.
Lincolnshire College of Art and Design, Lincoln.
Liverpool City College.
Loughborough College of Art and Design.
Loughton College of Further Education.
Lowestoft College.
Lurgan College of Further Education.
Mid-Cheshire College of Further Education, Northwich.
Nene College, Northampton.

Newcastle-under-Lyme College.
Newham Community College, London.
North Cheshire College, Warrington.
North Devon College, Barnstaple.
North East Wales Institute of Higher Education, Wrexham.
North Essex School of Art, Braintree.
North Essex School of Art (Colchester Institute).
Norfolk College of Art and Design, Norwich.
North Manchester College.
North Oxfordshire Technical College and School of Art, Banbury.
North Warwickshire College of Technology and Art, Nuneaton.
North West College of Technology, Londonderry.
North East Worcestershire College, Reddich.
Northbrook College of Design and Technology, Horsham and Worthing.
Norton College, Sheffield.
Parkwood College, Sheffield.
Plymouth College of Art and Design.
Pontypool College.
Richmond-upon-Thames College, Twickenham.
Rochdale College of Arts and Design.
Rotherham College of Arts and Technology.
Rupert Stanley College of Further Education, Belfast.
Salford College of Technology.
Shrewsbury College of Arts and Technology.
Solihull College of Technology.
Somerset College of Arts and Technology, Taunton.
South Devon College of Arts and Technology, Torquay.
South Nottinghamshire College of Further Education, West Bridgeford.
Southampton Institute of Higher Education.
Southend College of Technology.
Southport College of Art and Technology.
Southwark College, London.
Stafford College of Further Education.
Stourbridge College of Technology and Art.
Suffolk College of Higher and Further Education, Ipswich.
Sutton Coldfield College of Further Education.
Thurrock Technical College.
Trowbridge Technical College.
Wakefield District College.
Walsall College of Art.
West Glamorgan Institute of Higher Education, Swansea.
West Nottinghamshire College of Further Education, Mansfield.
Wigan College of Technology.
Worcester Technical College.
W. R. Tuson College, Preston.
York College of Arts and Technology.

Graphics – Advertising/Print
Barking College of Technology.
Bradford and Ilkley Community College.
Harlow College.
Kitson College of Technology, Leeds.
Liverpool City College.
London College of Printing (London Institute).
Nene College, Northampton.
Percival Whitley College of Further Education, Halifax.
Plymouth College of Art and Design.
South Fields College of Further Education, Leicester.
South Glamorgan Institute of Higher Education, Cardiff.
South Manchester Community College.
South Nottinghamshire College of Further Education, West Bridgeford.
Southampton Institute of Higher Education.
Watford College.
Wirral Metropolitan College, Wallasey.

Graphic Design/Visual Communication
Barnet College.
Barnfield College, Luton.
Barnsley College of Art and Design.
Berkshire College of Art and Design, Maidenhead.
Blackburn College of Technology and Design.
Blackpool and Fylde College of Further and Higher Education.
Bournemouth and Poole College of Art and Design, Poole.
Bournville College of Art, Birmingham.
Bradford and Ilkley Community College.
Brunel Technical College, Bristol.
Calderdale College.
Canterbury College of Art and Design (Kent Institute).
Chesterfield College of Technology and Arts.
Coventry Technical College.
Croydon College.
Derbyshire College of Higher Education, Derby.
Dewsbury College.
Doncaster Metropolitan Institute of Higher Education.
Dunstable College.
East Surrey College, Reigate.
Epsom School of Art and Design.
Falmouth School of Art and Design.
Farnborough College of Technology.
Gloucestershire College of Arts and Technology.
Guildford College of Technology.
Harlow College.
Harrogate College of Arts and Technology.
Hastings College of Arts and Technology.

Havering Technical College.
Hounslow Borough College.
Isle College, Wisbech.
Jacob Kramer College, Leeds.
Kingsway-Princeton College, London.
Kitson College of Technology, Leeds.
Lincolnshire College of Art and Design, Lincoln.
Loughborough College of Art and Design.
Loughton College of Further Education.
Lowestoft College.
Medway College of Art and Design (Kent Institute), Rochester.
Mid-Cheshire College of Further Education, Northwich.
Nene College, Northampton.
New College, Durham.
Newcastle-upon-Tyne College of Arts and Technology.
Newham Community College, London.
Norfolk College of Art and Design, Norwich.
North East Wales Institute of Higher Education, Wrexham.
North Essex School of Art (Colchester Institute).
Northbrook College of Design and Technology, Worthing.
Northumberland College of Arts and Technology, Ashington.
North Warwickshire College of Technology and Art, Nuneaton.
Norton College, Sheffield.
Parkwood College, Sheffield.
Plymouth College of Art and Design.
Portsmouth College of Art, Design and Further Education.
Rochdale College of Arts and Design.
Rotherham College of Arts and Technology.
Salford College of Technology.
Salisbury College of Art.
Scarborough Technical College.
Solihull College of Technology.
South Devon College of Arts and Technology, Torquay.
South Fields College of Further Education, Leicester.
South Manchester Community College.
South Nottinghamshire College of Further Education, West Bridgeford.
Southampton Institute of Higher Education.
Southport College of Art and Technology.
Stafford College of Further Education.
Stockport College of Technology.
Stourbridge College of Technology and Art.
Suffolk College of Higher and Further Education, Ipswich.
Sutton Coldfield College of Further Education.
Swindon College.
Tameside College of Technology.
Wakefield District College.
Walsall College of Art.

Ware College.
Watford College.
West Nottinghamshire College of Further Education, Mansfield.
Weston-super-Mare College of Further Education.
Wigan College of Technology.
Wirral Metropolitan College, Wallasey.
York College of Arts and Technology.

Graphics – Illustration/Technical Illustration
Barking College of Technology.
Blackburn College of Technology and Design.
Blackpool and Fylde College of Further and Higher Education.
Bournemouth and Poole College of Art and Design, Poole.
Bournville College of Art (Birmingham Institute of Art and Design).
Brunel Technical College, Bristol.
Doncaster Metropolitan Institute of Higher Education.
Falmouth School of Art and Design.
Isle College, Wisbech.
Mid-Cheshire College of Further Education, Northwich.
Mid-Warwickshire College of Further Education, Leamington Spa.
Portsmouth College of Art, Design and Further Education.
Ravensbourne College of Design and Communication, Chislehurst.
Southampton Institute of Higher Education.
West Glamorgan Institute of Higher Education, Swansea.

Industrial Design (Engineering)
Hounslow Borough College.
Kingsway-Princeton College, London.

Jewellery Design
Berkshire College of Art and Design, Maidenhead.
Bradford and Ilkley Community College.

Multi-disciplinary Design
These courses provide an opportunity to study two or more areas to the same level.
Bolton Institute of Higher Education. (Fashion/textile/three-dimensional design/graphic design.)
Carmarthenshire College of Technology and Art, Carmarthen. (Wildlife illustration/illustration/three-dimensional design/ceramics/fashion/textiles.)
Croydon College. (Design/three-dimensional design.)
Cumbria College of Art and Design, Carlisle. (Information from the college.)
Darlington College of Technology. (Information from the college.)
Falmouth School of Art and Design. (Information from the college.)

Herefordshire College of Art and Design, Hereford. (Constructed textiles/ jewellery/ceramics.)

Hertfordshire College of Art and Design (St. Albans School of Art and Design). (Three-dimensional design/graphic design/surface pattern design.)

Mid-Warwickshire College of Further Education, Leamington Spa. (Surface pattern/textiles/graphic design/three-dimensional craft and product design/fashion.)

Monkwearmouth College of Further Education. (Graphic design/textile/ fashion/three-dimensional design.)

Salford College of Technology. (Graphic design/spatial design/fashion.)

South Tyneside College, South Shields. (Graphic design/photography/ fashion/three-dimensional design/screen printing/visual studies.)

Southampton Institute of Higher Education. (Information from the college.)

Southwark College, London. (Graphic design/three-dimensional design/ fashion/textiles.)

Stevenage College. (Graphic design/product design/technical illustration/ fashion/textile.)

Stockport College of Technology. (Information from the college.)

Sutton Coldfield College of Further Education. (Information from the college.)

West Surrey College of Art and Design, Farnham. (Information from the college.)

Worcester Technical College. (Design/Graphic design.)

Photography

Barking College of Technology.
Barnfield College, Luton.
Berkshire College of Art and Design, Maidenhead.
Bournemouth and Poole College of Art and Design, Poole.
Bournville College of Art (Birmingham Institute of Art and Design).
Carmarthenshire College of Technology and Art, Carmarthen.
Crosskeys College.
Dewsbury College.
Harrogate College of Arts and Technology.
Herefordshire College of Art and Design, Hereford.
Kingsway-Princeton College, London.
Mid-Cheshire College of Further Education, Northwich.
Newcastle-upon-Tyne College of Arts and Technology.
Norton College, Sheffield.
Paddington College.
Parkwood College, Sheffield.
Plymouth College of Art and Design.
Sandwell College of Further and Higher Education.
South Nottinghamshire College of Further Education, West Bridgeford.
Southport College of Art and Technology.

Stockport College of Technology.
Ware College.
Watford College.
Wigan College of Technology.

Surface pattern design
Barnsley College of Art and Design.
Dewsbury College.
Parkwood College, Sheffield.
Norfolk College of Art and Design, Norwich.
Stockport College of Technology.

Textile design/embroidery/weave/tapestry
Bradford and Ilkley Community College.
Harrogate College of Arts and Technology.
London College of Fashion (London Institute).
London College of Furniture (City of London Polytechnic).
Northbrook College of Design and Technology, Worthing.

Theatre/stage design
Northbrook College of Design and Technology, Worthing.

Three-dimensional studies
These courses cover a wide range of design and manufacturing disciplines including product design, design for crafts and work in a range of materials including wood, metal and plastic.
Barnet College.
Berkshire College of Art and Design, Maidenhead.
Bournville College of Art (Birmingham Institute of Art and Design).
Chesterfield College of Technology and Arts.
Cleveland College of Art and Design, Middlesborough.
Cumbria College of Art and Design, Carlisle.
Doncaster Metropolitan Institute of Higher Education.
Harrogate College of Arts and Technology.
Kingsway-Princeton College, London.
Newcastle-upon-Tyne College of Arts and Technology.
North Essex School of Art (Colchester Institute).
North Worcestershire College, Redditch.
Northbrook College of Design and Technology, Worthing.
Parkwood College, Sheffield.
Portsmouth College of Art, Design and Further Education.
Southampton Institute of Higher Education.
Southwark College, London.
West Nottinghamshire College of Further Education, Mansfield.
Worcester Technical College.
York College of Arts and Technology.

Typography
Watford College.

BTEC First Diploma in Design
The following colleges offer this qualification which is awarded after successful completion of one year of full-time study. The minimum age at entry is sixteen years and there are no formal academic entry qualifications. It is normal practice for applicants to be asked to provide a portfolio of their art and design work at interview.
Aylesbury College.
Barking College of Technology.
Barnet College.
Barnfield College, Luton.
Barnsley College of Art and Design.
Basingstoke Technical College.
Bath College of Further Education.
Blackburn College of Technology and Design.
Boston College of Further Education.
Bradford and Ilkley Community College.
Brunel Technical College, Bristol. (Printing.)
Burnley College of Technology.
Cambridgeshire College of Arts and Technology, Cambridge.
Chesterfield College of Technology and Arts.
City and East London College.
Darlington College of Technology.
Dewsbury College.
East Surrey College, Reigate.
Falmouth School of Art and Design.
Haringey College, London.
Harlow College.
Harrogate College of Arts and Technology.
Herefordshire College of Art and Design, Hereford.
Hounslow Borough College.
Huddersfield Technical College.
Hull College of Further Education.
Jacob Kramer College, Leeds.
Kingsway College, London.
Kitson College, Leeds. (Printing.)
Lincolnshire College of Art, Lincoln.
Liverpool City College.
Loughton College of Further Education.
Lowestoft College of Further Education.
Mid-Cheshire College of Further Education, Northwich.
Mid-Warwickshire College of Further Education, Leamington Spa.
Nene College, Northampton.
Newcastle-under-Lyme College.
Newcastle-upon-Tyne College of Arts and Technology.

Newham Community College, London.
North Devon College, Barnstaple.
North East Wales Institute of Higher Education, Wrexham.
Northumberland Technical College, Ashington.
North Warwickshire College of Technology and Art, Nuneaton.
North East Worcestershire College, Redditch.
Norton College Sheffield.
Oxford College of Further Education.
Parkwood College, Sheffield.
Rochdale College of Arts and Design.
Rotherham College of Arts and Technology.
Salisbury College of Art.
Scarborough Technical College.
Solihull College of Further Education.
Southampton Technical College.
South Fields College of Further Education, Leicester.
South Manchester Community College.
Southport College of Art and Technology.
South Thames College, London.
South Tyneside College, South Shields.
Southwark College, London.
Stafford College of Further Education.
Stockport College of Technology.
Stourbridge College of Technology and Art.
Suffolk College of Higher and Further Education, Ipswich.
Sutton Coldfield College of Further Education.
Thanet Technical College, Broadstairs.
Thurrock Technical College, Grays.
Uxbridge Technical College.
Walsall College of Art.
Waltham Forest College, London.
Ware College.
Watford College.
West Nottinghamshire College of Further Education, Mansfield.
Wigan College of Technology.
Willesden College of Technology, London.
Wirral Metropolitan College, Wallasey.
Worcester Technical College.
York College of Arts and Technology.

National Council for Vocational Qualifications

The Council is responsible for the accreditation of a wide range and level of vocational qualifications awarded by bodies such as BTEC and the City and Guilds of London Institute. The approval of the Council follows the agreement of employers that the qualification meets the needs of industry and commerce at the level obtained by the student. In many cases the award is conditional on the student achieving a level of competence in the workplace as assessed during the period of work experience which is integral to the course. A National Vocational Qualification (NVQ) can be awarded at various levels depending on the skills and competences of the student. Increasing skills and competences can entitle the student to higher levels of award. The National Council do not make awards themselves. They accredit the awards of validating bodies.

Entry requirements

CNAA First Degree: art and design

All students are admitted to courses at the discretion of the institution providing the course. There must be a reasonable expectation that applicants will be able to fulfil the objectives of the course programme and achieve the standard required for the award. A wide range of formal qualifications and other forms of preparation provide a basis for admission including the General Certificate of Secondary Education (GCSE); General Certificate of Education at Advanced Level (GCE 'A' level) and BTEC National Diploma qualifications. In the selection of students for courses in art and design, the institutions expect the emphasis will normally be placed upon evidence of creative ability in art and design.

A student shall not normally be admitted to any full-time or sandwich course unless he or she has attained the age of eighteen years by 31 December in the year of entry. An institution may also exercise its discretion to admit a student whose qualifications do not conform to the standard minimum entrance requirements, but who presents other evidence which, in the opinion of the institution, indicates that he or she has the capacity and attainment to pursue the course of study proposed, provided that the proportion of students thus admitted is not so large as to affect significantly the nature and presentation of the course.

An institution may admit a mature student aged twenty-one years or over by 31 December in the year of entry, to the beginning of a course, not specifically designed for such a student, even when he or she does not possess the normal course entry qualifications, provided that the institution is first satisfied that the student has the necessary motivation, potential and knowledge to follow the course successfully.

BTEC courses

Higher Diploma: the appropriate BTEC Certificate or Diploma or equivalent qualifications.

Although the entry qualifications of the students may vary, the final BTEC awards gained have a common standard. The minimum age for entry to a Higher Diploma programme is eighteen years. In the majority of cases applicants for BTEC courses are required to provide a folio of work in art and design or other comparable evidence of achievement demonstrating potential for the course. In some cases students who have successfully completed a Foundation course may be eligible for entry to a Higher Diploma programme.

Some colleges will specify particular BTEC Diploma or Certificate awards as entry qualifications to their Higher Diploma programmes. It is therefore important that applicants should obtain from the colleges full details of the courses in which they are interested.

National Diploma: The length of programme is two years full-time and for admission to programmes usually four passes in the General Certificate of Secondary Education (GCSE) or equivalent are required but requirements vary – apply to colleges for detailed information.

Although the entry qualifications of the students may vary the final BTEC awards gained have a common standard. In the majority of cases applicants for BTEC courses in art and design are required to provide a folio of work in art and design or other comparable evidence of achievement demonstrating potential for the course. The normal, minimum age for entry to Diploma courses is sixteen years.

First Diploma: The length of programme is one year full-time and for admission to programme no formal academic qualifications are required. In the majority of cases all applicants for First Diploma places in art and design are required to submit a folio of recent work in art and design or other comparable evidence of achievement demonstrating potential for the course.

Certificate of Pre-Vocation Education: The length of programme is one year full-time and for admission to programme no formal academic qualifications are required. The programme of study allows choices to be made from a range of specialist subjects including design. Students who wish to specialise in design can do so on some courses. In such cases evidence of the recent art and design work of the applicant is normally required to be submitted at interview.

Finance whilst at college

Further Education Major Awards
Normally all students accepted for an unconditional place on a course leading to a Degree or a Higher National Diploma (HND) are entitled to apply for a mandatory award from their local education authority if they are resident in the United Kingdom and providing they fulfil certain conditions. Such courses are known as designated courses. Applications to local education authorities for the necessary forms should be made as early as possible. It is not necessary to wait for the offer of a place at university or college.

Students are financed at two possible levels:

1.   Tuition fees.   These are the fees payable for tuition at the university or college which accepts the student for a particular course. Normally these fees are paid direct by the local education authority.

2.   Maintenance Grant.   This is an award directly related to the income of the parent(s) of students who are not self-supporting. It is based on a scale of residual income after certain deductions. A similar method of calculation is used for the assessment of students who are financially independent. The level of mandatory awards is to be pegged by the Government and a scheme of loans introduced to compensate for the difference.

Further Education Discretionary Awards
Most local education authorities make a number of discretionary awards for certain courses outside the regulations governing mandatory awards. Applications for these awards should be made direct to your local education authority as soon as possible before you are committed to a course. In some cases a discretionary award may be made where the applicant is debarred from receiving a mandatory award. Some authorities may be willing to make an award for a place at an independent college.

Note.   Both mandatory and discretionary awards are provided to cover the cost of accommodation, travel and all other support costs during term time. The parental contribution with or without the award is judged on the expected costs of the maintenance of the student for one academic year.

Many colleges now make an annual studio fee or similar charge for art and design students. This is to help students offset the high cost of providing specialist materials individually. Bulk buying by the institution is a means of saving the student unnecessary additional expense. Art and Design is an expensive area. The cost of materials must be borne in mind when assessing course costs.

4.2 GLOSSARY

Art and design

Airbrush A device for spraying paint with compressed air.
Art Nouveau Nineteenth-century ornamental art-style.
Assemblage A three-dimensional form made from two or more
    components.
Collage A work put together by the assembly of individual, two-
    dimensional or three-dimensional elements.

Contour The edge or edges of an object, normally, but not necessarily, three-dimensional.

Composition The bringing together of several elements to make a whole.

Display type Displayed typesetting, such as title-pages, advertisements, etc. distinguished from solid text setting.

End grain A cross-section of timber. Used for wood engraving.

Ergonomics The study of work in relation to the environment in which it is performed.

Fine art Painting, sculpture, etc. – work of a non-utilitarian nature in which mind and imagination are chiefly concerned.

Floppy disk Flexible disk coated with a magnetic substance used to store data for a computer.

Form As in 'human form'. The visual relationship between two or more three-dimensional shapes.

Half-tone Representation of light and shade photographically by dots of different sizes. Used for all the usual printing methods.

Hologram A means of optical imaging without the use of lenses, now a practical reality with the advent of the laser (see below).

House style The customary style of spelling, capitalisation, etc. followed in a printing or publishing establishment.

Laser Light Amplification by Stimulated Emission of Radiation. A coherent light source using a crystalline solid (e.g. ruby) liquid or gas-discharge tube, in which atoms are pumped simultaneously into excited states by an incoherent light flash.

Line As in 'line drawing'. An idea or observation expressed by a drawn line without the use of tone (shading).

Logo Shortened form of 'logotype', a word or several letters cast in one piece of type, or presented as a trade mark.

Mass Large undefined shape. Usually three-dimensional.

Microprocessor A very small computer (composed of one or more integrated circuits functioning as a unit).

Monochrome Work in a number of tones of the same colour.

Monoprint A single colour print.

Nodal point Usually a drawing which plots the surface of an object with changes in direction shown as points, dots or nodes.

Object-trouve Found objects utilised as artefacts by being incorporated into an art work.

Offset printing Process in which the ink from a plate is received on a rubber-covered blanket cylinder, from which it is transferred to the paper or other material.

Pattern Usually associated with surface design. Can be regular or irregular, two-or three-dimensional.

Photogram Photographic image made direct on to photographic paper without the use of a negative.

Plane A flat, level surface.

Portfolio A collection of drawings, prints, etc.

Rag-mould Paper making process utilising rag.

Resist A coating of chemically neutral substance placed over a surface when the latter has to be protected at some stage of processing as in etching or selective dyeing.

Reverse printing Where the negative image is reversed in processing to give a positive image.

Scale Size, in relation to other objects.

Silhouette An object or person viewed two-dimensionally and drawn without variation in colour or tone.

Software General term for programming or compiling accessories used for computing or data-processing systems.

Source material Original material used to develop an idea.

Space The three-dimensional area between two or more defined forms.

Structure The underlying components which influence the external appearance.

Tactile The 'feel' or texture of a surface when the response is not gained from actually touching but by being conscious of the nature of the texture.

Tension breaker Liquid for increasing the flow of acrylic colours on non-absorbent surface.

Texture Surface quality, i.e. rough, smooth, wet, oily, prickly, etc.

Tone As 'tone drawing'. An idea or observation expressed in gradations of one or more colours.

Toothed surface Roughened surface, usually to paper.

Trichromatic separation Three-colour separation.

Volume The extent of a three-dimensional space occupied or enclosed within an object.

4.3 PAPER SIZES

International standard paper sizes

The three basic sheets of the international standard series are known as 'A', 'B' and 'C', which are related by a common dimensional ratio extending from 'A' to the larger sheets 'B' and 'C'. Sizes obtained from subdivisions of these sheets are designated by numerals following the sheet letter (A4, B6, C2, etc). Each numeral indicates a halving of the previous area. Thus, A1 is half, A2 a quarter and A3 an eighth of the A sheet area, and so on. Full sheet sizes are coded A0, B0, C0. For still larger sizes, the numeral is prefixed to the letter. Thus, 2A is twice the size of A0.

The 'A' Series (illustrated below) is designed for all standard printing and stationery purposes – that is, for the whole range of printed forms, catalogues and periodicals, and for all administrative, commercial and technical documents or letterheads.

Dimensions of 'A' sheet sizes are listed below. Note that these are all *trimmed* sizes, which ensures consistency of supply however many different suppliers are involved.

	millimetres	*inches (approx.)*
A0	841 × 1189	33⅛ × 46¾
A1	594 × 841	23⅜ × 33⅛
A2	420 × 594	16½ × 23⅜
A3	297 × 420	11¾ × 16½
A4	210 × 297	8¼ × 11¾
A5	148 × 210	5⅞ × 8¼
A6	105 × 148	4⅛ × 5⅞
A7	74 × 105	2⅞ × 4⅛

Imperial paper sizes

crown	15 × 20 in
demy	17½ × 22½ in
foolscap	17 × 13½ in
Imperial	22 × 30 in
medium	18 × 23 in
post	12½ × 15½ in
royal	20 × 25 in
small royal	25 × 19 in

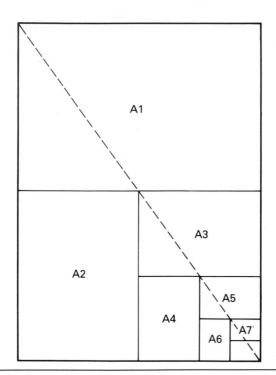

Fig. 4.1

4.4 METRIC/IMPERIAL MEASUREMENTS AND EQUIVALENTS

Table 4.1 Metric/imperial measures

Metric measures and equivalents		Imperial measures and equivalents	
Length		*Length*	
1 millimetre (mm)	= 10 mm	1 inch	= 2.54 cm
1 centimetre (cm)	= 100 cm	1 foot (ft)	= 12 in	= 0.3048 m
1 metre (m)	= 1,000 m	1 yard (yd)	= 3 ft	= 0.9144 m
1 kilometre (km)		1 mile	= 1,760 yd	= 1.6093 km
Area		*Area*	
1 sq cm (cm²)	= 100 mm² = 0.1550 in²	1 sq inch (in²)	= 6.4516 cm²
1 sq metre (m²)	= 10,000 cm² = 1.1960 yd²	1 sq foot (ft²)	= 144 in²	= 0.0929 m²
1 sq km (km²)	= 100 hectares = 0.3861 mile²	1 sq yard (yd²)	= 9 ft²	= 0.8361 m²
		1 acre	= 4,840 yd²	= 4046.9 m²
		1 sq mile (mile²)	= 640 acres	= 2.590 km²
Volume/Capacity		*Volume/Capacity*	
1 cu. cm (cm³)	= 0.0610 in³	1 cu inch (in³)	= 16.387 cm³
1 cu. decimetre (dm³)	= 1,000 cm³ = 0.0353 ft³	1 cu foot (ft³)	= 1,728 in³	= 0.0283 m³
1 cu. metre (m³)	= 1,000 dm³ = 1,3080 yd³	1 cu yard (yd³)	= 27 ft³	= 0.7646 m³
1 litre (l)	= 1 dm³ = 1.76 pt	1 fluid ounce (fl oz)	= 28.413 ml
	= 2.113 US 1 pt	1 pint (pt)	= 20 fl oz	= 0.58631
1 hectolitre (hl)	= 100 l = 21.997 gal	1 gallon (gal)	= 8 pt	= 4.5461
	= 26.417 US gal		
Mass (Weight)		*Mass (Weight)*	
1 milligram (mg)	= 0.0154 grain	1 ounce (oz)	= 437.5 grains	= 28.35 g
1 gram (g)	= 1,000 mg = 0.0353 oz	1 pound (lb)	= 16 oz	= 0.4536 kg
1 metric carat	= 0.2 g = 3.0865 grains	1 stone	= 14 lb	= 6.3503 kg
1 kilogram (kg)	= 1,000 g = 2.2046 lb	1 hundredweight (cwt)	= 112 lb	= 50.802 kg
1 tonne (t)	= 1,000 kg = 0.9842 ton	1 ton	= 20 cwt	= 1.016 t
	= 1.1023 short ton		

Table 4.2   Approximate equivalents

Length			Mass (Weight)		
centimetres (cm)		inches (in)	kilograms (kg)		pounds (lb)
2.54	1	0.394	0.454	1	2.205
5.08	2	0.787	0.907	2	4.409
7.62	3	1.181	1.361	3	6.614
10.16	4	1.575	1.814	4	8.819
12.70	5	1.969	2.268	5	11.023
15.24	6	2.362	2.722	6	13.228
17.78	7	2.756	3.175	7	15.432
20.32	8	3.150	3.629	8	17.637
22.86	9	3.543	4.082	9	19.842
25.40	10	3.937	4.536	10	22.046
50.80	20	7.874	9.072	20	44.092
76.20	30	11.811	13.608	30	66.139
101.60	40	15.748	18.144	40	88.185
127.00	50	19.685	22.680	50	110.231
152.40	60	23.622	27.216	60	132.277
177.80	70	27.559	31.752	70	154.324
203.20	80	31.496	36.287	80	176.370
228.60	90	35.433	40.823	90	198.416
254.00	100	39.370	45.359	100	220.462

Length			Volume		
kilometres (km)		miles	litres		UK gallons
1.609	1	0.621	4.546	1	0.220
3.219	2	1.243	9.092	2	0.440
4.828	3	1.864	13.638	3	0.660
6.437	4	2.485	18.184	4	0.880
8.047	5	3.107	22.730	5	1.100
9.656	6	3.728	27.276	6	1.320
11.265	7	4.350	31.822	7	1.540
12.875	8	4.971	36.368	8	1.760
14.484	9	5.592	40.914	9	1.980
16.093	10	6.214	45.460	10	2.200
32.187	20	12.427	90.919	20	4.399
48.280	30	18.641	136.379	30	6.599
64.374	40	24.855	181.839	40	8.799
80.467	50	31.069	227.298	50	10.998
96.561	60	37.282	272.758	60	13.198
112.654	70	43.496	318.217	70	15.398
128.748	80	49.710	363.677	80	17.598
144.841	90	55.923	409.137	90	19.797
160.934	100	62.137	454.596	100	21.997

4.5   BIBLIOGRAPHY

Books

(a) Painting

Doerner, M. (1969) *The Materials of the Artist*. Harrap, London.
Kay, R. (1961) *The Painters' Guide to Studio Methods and Materials*. Studio Vista, London; Doubleday, New York.

(b) Colour

Birren, F. (Ed.) 1970. *The Elements of Colour* (Itten). Van Nostrand Reinhold, New York.

(c) Sculpture
Mills, J. (1976) *The Techniques of Sculpture*. Batsford, London.

(d) Print-making
Gilmour, P. (1981) *Artists in Print*. BBC Publications.
Heller, J. (1972) *Printmaking Today*. Holt, Rinehart & Winston, New York.
Mara, T. (1979) *Screen Printing*. Thames & Hudson, London.
Vicary, R. (1976) *Lithography*. Thames & Hudson, London.

(e) Graphic design
Craig, J. (1974) *Production for the Graphic Designer*. Pitman Publishing, London; Watson-Guptill Publications, New York.
Garland, K. (1966) *Graphics Handbook*. Studio Vista, London; Reinhold, New York.
Garland, K. (1980) *Illustrated Graphics Glossary*. Barrie & Jenkins, London.
Hurlburt, A. (1977) *Layout – The Design of the Printed Page*. Barrie & Jenkins, London; Watson-Guptill Publications, New York.
Hurlburt, A. (1978) *The Grid*. Van Nostrand Reinhold, New York.
Lewis, J. (1977) *Typography – Design and Practice*. Barrie & Jenkins, London.

(f) Photography
Feininger, A. (1978) *The Complete Photographer*. Thames & Hudson, London.
J. Hedgecoe and M. J. Langford (1971) *Photography – Materials and Methods*. Oxford University Press.
Horder, A. (Ed.) (1971) *Manual of Photography*. Lund Humphries, London; Focal Press, New York.
Langford, M. J. (1977) *Basic Photography*. Focal Press.

(g) Fashion
J. Arnold (1972) *Patterns of Fashion*. Macmillan, London; Drama Books Specialists, USA.

(h) Textiles
Dushemin, M. (1975) *Handweaving*. Batsford, London.
Hardingham, M. (1978) *The Illustrated Dictionary of Fabrics*. Studio Vista/Cassell, London; Collier-Macmillan, New York.
Russ, S. (1964) *Fabric Printing by Hand*. Studio Vista, London; Watson-Guptill Publications, New York.
Storey, J. (1974) *Textile Printing*. Thames & Hudson, London.

(i) Ceramics
M. Billington and J. Colbeck (1974) *The Techniques of Pottery*. Batsford, London.

(j) Jewellery/silversmithing

Brynner, I. (1968) *Modern Jewelry*. Van Nostrand Reinhold, New York.
Gentille, T. (1973) *Jewellery*. Evans Bros., London.
Smith, K. (1975) *Practical Silversmithing and Jewelry*. Studio Vista,
   London.

(k) Art and design history

Clark, K. (1949) *Landscape into Art*. John Murray, London.
Gombrich, E. H. (1950) *The Story of Art*. Phaidon, London.
Murray, P. and L. (1959) *A Dictionary of Art and Artists*. Penguin Books,
   Harmondsworth.
Wilenski, R. H. (1940) *Modern French Painters*. Faber & Faber,
   London.
Wolfflin, H. (1952) *Classic Art*. Phaidon, London.

Monographs and series

There are a number of very good monographs on the work of individual
artists, and also books dealing with the major periods of art history or
aspects of the art of countries and continents which are usually available
as part of a series of books published over a period of time.

The following series are particularly recommended for the quality of
the reproductions.

Hofstatter, H. (Gen. Ed.) *Panorama of World Art Series*. Harry N.
   Abrams, London, New York. Titles available include: *Art of the Late
   Middle Ages*; *Pre-Columbian Art and Later Indian Tribal Art*; *African
   and Oceanic Art*; *Art of the Far East*; *Baroque and Rococo Art*;
   Renaissance and Mannerist Art.
H. Jaffe and Busignani (Gen. Eds.) *Twentieth Century Masters Series*.
   Hamlyn.
Lecaidano, P. (Ed.) *Classics of World Art Series*. Weidenfeld and
   Nicolson, London; Harry N. Abrams, New York.
Phaidon *Colour Plate Series*.
Skira Series, *The Treasures of Asia* and *Great Centuries of Painting*. Some
   titles are also available in a new edition published by Macmillan.
The *World of Art Library*. Thames & Hudson, London.

Visual research

Betjeman, J. (Ed.) (1979) *Collins Guide to Parish Churches of England
   and Wales*. Collins, London.
R. Fedden and J. Kenworthy-Brown (1979) *The Country House Guide*.
   Jonathan Cape, London.
Fry, P. S. (1980) *The David and Charles Book of Castles*, David &
   Charles, Newton Abbot.
Pevsner, N. (Founding Ed.) *The Buildings of England* (Series). Penguin
   Books, Harmondsworth.

Museum and Galleries in Great Britain and Ireland. Published annually by ABC Historic Publications.

Periodicals

Audio-visual
Audio-Visual Monthly.

Ceramics
Ceramic Review, bi-monthly.

Design
The Architectural Review, monthly; *Domus* (Italy), monthly; *Design Magazine* (UK), monthly.

Fashion
Fashion Weekly; *Robes Couture* (France), twice yearly; *Vogue UK*, monthly.

Film
British Film Institute Monthly Film Bulletin; *Framework*, quarterly; *Sight and Sound*, quarterly.

Fine arts
Art forum (USA), monthly; *Art International* (Swiss), five per year; *Art Monthly* (UK); *Artscribe* (UK), bi-monthly; *Arts Review* (UK), fortnightly; *Studio International* (UK), quarterly.

Graphic design
Campaign (UK), weekly; *Communication Arts* (USA), bi-monthly; *Graphics* (Swiss), bi-monthly.

Photography
British Journal of Photography, weekly; *Creative Camera*, monthly.

College courses

Higher Education in the UK. A handbook for students from overseas and their advisors. Longman Group Ltd, for the Association of Commonwealth Universities and British Council.

A Compendium of Advanced Courses in Colleges of Further and Higher Education. London and Home Counties Regional Advisory Council for Technological Education, Tavistock House South, Tavistock Square, London, WC1H 9LR.

CNAA Directory of First Degree and Diploma of Higher Education Courses. Council for National Academic Awards, 344–354 Gray's Inn Road, London, WC1X 8BP.

Polytechnic Courses Handbook. Published by the Committee of Directors of Polytechnics, 309 Regent Street, London, W1R 7PE.
The Handbook of Degree and Advanced Courses in Institutes, Colleges of Higher Education, Colleges of Education, Polytechnics and University Departments of Education. Lund Humphries, The Country Press, Drummond Road, Bradford, BD8 8DH.

4.6   USEFUL ADDRESSES

Suppliers. The following firms are manufacturers, agents, wholesalers or importers of items mentioned in this handbook or of similar items. The majority of local art and design materials stockists in the United Kingdom will be able to supply specific items, but in case of difficulty or when certain specialist items are required it may be necessary to contact the suppliers whose names, addresses and telephone numbers are listed below.

General art and design

Berol Ltd,
Oldmeadow Road, King's Lynn, Norfolk, PE30 4JR.
Tel: 0553 61221

Caran D'Ache,
Jakar International Ltd, Hillside House, 2–6 Friern Park, London, N12 9BX.
Tel: 081 445 6377

A. W. Faber-Castell (UK) Ltd,
Crompton Road, Stevenage, Herts, SG1 2EF.
Tel: 0438 316511

Reeves,
Whitefriars Avenue,
Wealdstone, Harrow, Middlesex, HA3 5RH.
Tel: 081 427 4343

Staedtler (UK) Ltd,
Pontyclun, Mid-Glamorgan, Wales, CF7 8YJ.
Tel: 0443 237421

Winsor & Newton,
Wealdstone, Harrow, Middlesex, HA3 5RH.
Tel: 081 427 4343

Specialist suppliers

Boards/papers/sketch-blocks/pads
Daler-Rowney Ltd,
Southern Industrial Area,
PO Box 10, Bracknell, Berkshire, RG12 4ST.
Tel: 0344 424621

Frisk Ltd,
4 Franthorne Way, Randlesdown Road, London, SE6 3BT.
Tel: 081 698 3481

Oram & Robinson Ltd,
Cadmore Lane, Cheshunt, Waltham Cross, Hertfordshire, EN8
9SG.
Tel: 0992 27376

Slater Harrison & Co Ltd,
Lowerhouse Mills, West Bollington, Macclesfield, SK10 5HW.
Tel: 0625 73155

Paper retailers – London
Paper Point (Wiggins Teape Ltd),
63 Poland Street, London, W1.
Tel: 071 439 4414

Paperchase Products Ltd,
213 Tottenham Court Road, London, W1.
Tel: 071 580 8496

Printmaking suppliers
Daler-Rowney,
Westminster Road, Wareham, Dorset, BH20 4SW.
Tel: 09295 6621

Hunter Penrose Ltd,
7 Spa Road, London, SE16.
Tel: 071 407 5051

T. N. Lawrence & Son Ltd,
Bleeding Hart Yard, Greville Street, Hatton Garden, London,
EC1N 8SL.
Tel: 071 242 3534

Process Supplies Ltd,
19 Mount Pleasant, London, WC1.
Tel: 071 837 2179

Sericol Ltd,
26 Parsons Green Lane, London, SW6.
Tel: 071 736 3388

Graphic design

C. W. Edding (UK) Ltd,
Merlin Centre,
Acrewood Way, St. Albans, Herts, AJ4 0JY.
Tel: 0727 34471

Royal Sovereign Ltd.
6/7 St Georges' Industrial Estate,
White Hart Lane, London, N22 5QL.
Tel: 081 888 7029

West Design Products Ltd,
(UNO/Schoellershammer/Maped products)
684 Mitcham Road, Croydon CR9 3AB.
Tel: 081 684 6171

Photography

Kodak Ltd,
(Customer Relations), PO Box 66, Station Road, Hemel
Hempstead, Herts, HP1 1JU.
Tel: 0442 61122

Three-dimensional design

Ceramics
Clayglaze Ltd,
Kings Yard Pottery, Talbot Road, Rickmansworth, Herts.
Tel: 0923 87107

Wengers Ltd,
Etruria, Stoke-on-Trent, ST4 7BQ.
Tel: 0782 25560

Jewellery/Silversmithing
Copper: J. Smith & Sons, Ltd,
50 St John's Square, London, EC1.
Tel: 071 253 1277

Engravers: Guill & Stephenson,
Penny Bank Chambers, St John's Square, EC1.
Tel: 071 250 0651

Goldsmiths Hall: Foster Lane, London, EC2.
Tel: 071 606 8971

Jewellery tools: Walsh & Gray Ltd,
12–16 Clerkenwell Road, EC1 and 243 Beckenham Road, Kent,
BR3 4TS.
Tel: 081 778 7061

Perspex: R. Denny & Co. Ltd,
13–15 Netherwood Road, London, W14.
Tel: 071 603 5152

Plastic: G. H. Bloore Ltd,
480 Honeypot Lane, Stanmore, Middlesex.
Tel: 081 952 2391

Silver: Johnson Matthey,
43 Hatton Garden, EC1.
Tel: 071 405 6959

Silversmithing tools: Cooper Bros. & Sons, Ltd,
Mosley House, Holborn Viaduct, London, EC1.
Tel: 071 353 3865

Stones: C. Calipe,
44 Poland Street, London, W1.
Tel: 071 437 6534

College addresses

Accrington and Rossendale College, Sandy Lane, Accrington, BB5 2AW.
  Tel: 0254 393521.
Amersham College of Further Education, Art and Design, Stanley Hill,
  Amersham, HP7 9HN. Tel: 0494 721121.
Aylesbury College, Oxford Road, Aylesbury, HP21 8PD.Tel: 0296
  434111.
Barking College of Technology, Dagenham Road, Romford, RM7 0XU.
  Tel: 0708 766841.
Barnet College, Wood Street, Barnet, EN5 4AZ. Tel: 081 440 6321.
Barnfield College, New Bedford Road, Luton, LU3 2AX. Tel: 0582
  507531.
Barnsley College of Art and Design, Churchfield, Barnsley, S70 2BH.
  Tel: 0226 285623.
Basingstoke Technical College, Worthing Road, Basingstoke, Hampshire,
  RG21 1TN. Tel: 0256 54141.

Bath College of Further Education, Avon Street, Bath, BA1 1UP. Tel: 0225 312191.

Bath College of Higher Education (incorporating Bath Academy of Art), Newton Park, Newton St. Loe, Bath, BA2 9BN. Tel: 0225 873701.

Bedford College of Higher Education, Cauldwell Street, Bedford, MK42 9AH. Tel: 0234 45151.

Belfast College of Technology, College Square East, Belfast, BT1 6DJ. Tel: 0232 227244.

Berkshire College of Art and Design, Raymond Road, Maidenhead, SL6 6DF. Tel: 0628 24302.

Birmingham Institute of Art and Design (City of Birmingham Polytechnic), Gosta Green, Birmingham, B4 7DX. Tel: 021 331 5810.

Blackburn College of Technology and Design, Feilden Street, Blackburn, BB2 1LH. Tel: 0254 55144.

Blackpool and Fylde College of Further and Higher Education, Ashfield Road, Bispham, Blackpool, FY2 0HB. Tel: 0253 52352.

Bolton Institute of Higher Education, Deane Road, Bolton, BL3 5AB. Tel: 0204 28851.

Boston College of Further Education, Rowley Road, Boston, PE21 6JF. Tel: 0205 65701.

Bournemouth and Poole College of Art and Design, Wallisdown Road, Wallisdown, Poole, BH12 5HH. Tel: 0202 533011.

Bournville College of Art (see *Birmingham Institute of Art and Design*)

Bradford and Ilkley Community College, Great Horton Road, Bradford, West Yorkshire, BD7 1AY. Tel: 0274 753026.

Bretton Hall College, West Bretton, Wakefield, West Yorkshire, WF4 4L9. Tel: 092 485 261.

Brighton Polytechnic, Moulsecoomb, Brighton, BN2 4AT. Tel: 0273 693655.

Bristol Polytechnic, Coldharbour Lane, Frenchay, Bristol, BS16 1QY. Tel: 0272 656261.

Brunel Technical College, Ashley Down, Bristol, BS7 9BU. Tel: 0272 41241.

Buckinghamshire College of Higher Education, Queen Alexandra Road, High Wycombe, HP11 2JZ. Tel: 0494 22141.

Burnley College of Technology, Shorey Bank, Ormerod Road, Burnley, BB11 2RX. Tel: 0282 36111.

Calderdale College, Francis Street, Halifax, HX1 3UZ. Tel: 0422 58221.

Camberwell School of Art and Crafts (London Institute), Peckham Road, London, SE5 8UF. Tel: 071 703 0987.

Cambridgeshire College of Arts and Technology, East Road, Cambridge, CB1 1PT. Tel: 0223 63271.

Canterbury College of Art and Design (Kent Institute), New Dover Road, Canterbury, CT1 3AN. Tel: 0227 769371.

Carmarthenshire College of Technology and Art, Alban Road, Llanelli, SA15 1NG. Tel: 0554 759165.

Cassio College, Langley Road, Watford, WD1 3RH. Tel: 0923 240311.

Cauldon College of Further and Higher Education, Stoke Road, Shelton, Stoke-on-Trent, ST4 2DG. Tel: 0782 202561.

Central London Polytechnic, 309 Regent Street, London, W1R 8AL. Tel: (Admissions) 071 486 5811.

Central Manchester College, Taylor Street, Gorton, Greater Manchester, M18 8DF. Tel: 061 223 8282.

Central School of Art and Design (London Institute), Southampton Row, London, WC18 4AP. Tel: 071 405 1825.

Central School of Speech and Drama, Embassy Theatre, Eton Avenue, London, NW3 3HY. Tel: 071 722 8183.

Chelsea School of Art (London Institute), Manresa Road, London, SW3 6LS. Tel: 071 351 3844.

Chester College of Further Education, Blacon Avenue, Blacon, Chester, Cheshire, CH1 5PD. Tel: 0244 377595.

Chesterfield College of Technology and Arts, Infirmary Road, Chesterfield, S41 7NG. Tel: 0246 31212.

City and East London College, Jubilee Street, London, E1 0PT. Tel: 071 790 1066.

City of Birmingham Polytechnic, Corporation Street, Gosta Green, Birmingham. Tel: 021 331 5800.

City of London Polytechnic, 117 Houndsditch, London, EC3A 7BU. Tel: 071 283 1030.

Cleveland College of Art and Design, Green Lane, Middlesbrough, TS5 7RJ. Tel: 0642 821441.

Colchester Institute, Sheepen Road, Colchester, CO3 3LL. Tel: 0206 761660.

College for the Distributive Trades (London Institute), 30 Leicester Square, London, WC2H 7LE. Tel: 071 839 1547.

Cordwainers Technical College (City of London), 182 Mare Street, Hackney, London, E8 3RE. Tel: 081 985 0273.

Coventry Technical College, The Butts, Coventry, CV1 3GD. Tel: 0203 257221.

Coventry (Lanchester) Polytechnic, Priory Street, Coventry, CV1 5FB. Tel: 0203 631313.

Crewe and Alsager College of Higher Education, Crewe Road, Crewe, CW1 1DU. Tel: 0270 500661.

Crosskeys College, Crosskeys, Gwent, NP1 7ZA. Tel: 0495 270295.

Croydon College, Fairfield, Croydon, CR9 1DX. Tel: 081 686 5700.

Cumbria College of Art and Design, Brampton Road, Carlisle, CA3 9AY. Tel: 0228 25333.

Dacorum College, Marlowes, Hemel Hempstead, HP1 1HD. Tel: 0442 63771.

Darlington College of Technology, Cleveland Avenue, Darlington, DL3 7BB. Tel: 0325 467651.

Dartington College of Arts, Totnes, Devon, TO9 6EJ. Tel: 0803 862224.

Derbyshire College of Higher Education, Kedleston Road, Derby, DE3 1GB. Tel: 0332 47181.

Dewsbury College, Halifax Road, Dewsbury, WF13 2AS.
  Tel: 0924 465916.
Doncaster Metropolitan Institute of Higher Education, Waterdale,
  Doncaster, DN1 3EX. Tel: 0302 22122.
Duncan of Jordanstone College of Art, Perth Road, Dundee, DD1 4HT.
  Tel: 0382 23261.
Dunstable College, Kingsway, Dunstable, LU5 4HG. Tel: 0582 696451.
Eastbourne College of Arts and Technology, St. Anne's Road, Eastbourne,
  BN21 2HS. Tel: 0323 644711.
East Surrey College, Blackborough Road, Reigate, RH2 7DE.
  Tel: 0737 766661.
East Warwickshire College of Further Education, Lower Hillmorton Road,
  Rugby, CV21 3QS. Tel: 0788 73133.
Epsom School of Art and Design, Ashley Road, Epsom, KT18 5BE.
  Tel: 0372 728811.
Erith College of Technology, Tower Road, Belvedere, Kent, DA17 6JA.
  Tel: 0322 442331.
Exeter Faculty of Art and Design (Polytechnic of the South-West), Earl
  Richards Road North, Exeter, EX2 6AS. Tel: 0392 77977.
Falmouth School of Art and Design, Woodland, Falmouth, TR11 4RA.
  Tel: 0326 211077.
Farnborough College of Technology, Boundary Road, Farnborough,
  GU14 6SB. Tel: 0252 515511.
Glasgow School of Art, 167 Renfrew Street, Glasgow, G3 6RQ.
  Tel: 041 332 9797.
Gloucestershire College of Arts and Technology, Oxstalls Lane, Gloucester,
  GL2 9HW. Tel: 0452 426700.
Goldsmiths' College, New Cross, London, SE14 6NW.
  Tel: 081 692 7171.
Grimsby College of Technology, Nuns Corner, Grimsby, DN34 5BQ.
  Tel: 0472 79292.
Guildford College of Technology, Stoke Park, Guildford, GU1 1EZ.
  Tel: 0483 31251.
Gwent College of Higher Education, College Crescent, Caerleon,
  Newport, NP6 1XJ. Tel: 0633 421292.
Gwynedd Technical College, Ffriddoed Road, Bangor, Gwynedd, LL59
  5DY. Tel: 0248 362122.
Halton College of Further Education, Kingsway, Widnes, WA8 7QQ.
  Tel: 051 423 1391.
Handsworth Technical College, The Council House, Soho Road,
  Handsworth, Birmingham, B21 9DP. Tel: 021 551 6031.
Haringey College, Park Road, Bounds Green, London, N11 2QF.
  Tel: 081 888 7123.
Harrow College of Higher Education, Northwick Park, Harrow, HA1
  3TP. Tel: 081 864 5422.
Havering Technical College, Ardleigh Green Road, Hornchurch, RM11
  2LL. Tel: 0402 455011.

Harlow College, College Square, The High, Harlow, CM20 1LT.
Tel: 0279 441288.
Harrogate College of Arts and Technology, Hornbeam Park, Hookstone
Road, Harrogate, HG2 8QT. Tel: 0423 879466.
Hastings College of Arts and Technology, Archery Road, St-Leonards-on-
Sea, East Sussex, TN38 0HX. Tel: 0424 423847.
Herefordshire College of Art and Design, Folly Lane, Hereford, HR1
1LT. Tel: 0432 273359.
Hertfordshire College of Art and Design, 7 Hatfield Road, St. Albans, AL1
3RS. Tel: 0727 64414.
Highbury College of Technology, Cosham, Portsmouth, PO6 2SA.
Tel: 0705 383131.
Hinckley College of Further Education, London Road, Hinckley, LE10
1HQ. Tel: 0455 632388.
Hounslow Borough College, London Road, Isleworth, Middlesex, TW7
4HS. Tel: 081 568 0244.
Huddersfield Polytechnic, Queensgate, Huddersfield, HD1 3DH.
Tel: 0484 22288.
Huddersfield Technical College, New North Road, Huddersfield, HD1
5NN. Tel: 0484 536521.
Hull College of Further Education, Queen's Gardens, Hull, HU1 3DG.
Tel: 0482 29943.
Humberside College of Higher Education, Cottingham Road, Hull, HU6
7RT. Tel: 0482 41451.
Isle College, Ramnoth Road, Wisbech, PE13 2JE. Tel: 0945 582561.
Jacob Kramer College, Vernon Street, Leeds, LS2 8PH.
Tel: 0532 439931.
Kidderminster College of Further Education, Hoo Road, Kidderminster,
DY10 1LX. Tel: 0562 820811.
Kilburn Polytechnic, Priory Park Road, London, NW6 1YB.
Tel: 071 328 8241.
Kingston College of Further Education, Kingston Hall Road, Kingston
upon Thames, KT1 2AQ. Tel: 081 546 2151.
Kingston Polytechnic, Penrhyn Road, Kingston upon Thames, KT1
2EE. Tel: 081 549 1366.
Kingsway College, Grays Inn Centre, Sidmouth Street, London, WC1H
8JB. Tel: 071 278 0541.
Kitson College of Technology, Cookridge Street, Leeds, LS2 8BL.
Tel: 0532 430381.
Lancaster and Morecombe College of Further Education, Morecombe
Road, Lancaster, LA1 2TY. Tel: 0524 66215.
Lancashire Polytechnic, Preston, PR1 2TQ. Tel: 0772 22141.
Leeds Polytechnic, Calverley Street, Leeds, LS1 9BH. Tel: 0532 462934.
Leicester Polytechnic, PO Box 143, Leicester, LE1 9BH.
Tel: 0533 551551.
Leigh College, Conston Street, Leigh, Greater Manchester, WN7 1XN.
Tel: 0942 608811.

Lincolnshire College of Art and Design, Lindum Road, Lincoln, LN2
1NP. Tel: 0522 23268.
Liverpool City College, Myrtle Street, Liverpool, L1 7DN.
Tel: 051 708 0423.
Liverpool Institute of Higher Education, Stand Park Road, Liverpool, L16
9JD. Tel: 051 722 2361.
Liverpool Polytechnic, 68 Hope Street, Liverpool, L1 9EB.
Tel: 051 207 3581.
Llandrillo Technical College, Llandudno Road, Colwyn Bay, LL28 4HZ.
Tel: 0492 46666.
London College of Fashion (London Institute), 20 John Prince's Street,
London, W1M 9HE. Tel: 071 629 9401.
London College of Furniture (City of London Polytechnic), 41–71
Commercial Road, London, E1 1LA. Tel: 071 247 1953.
London College of Printing (London Institute), Elephant & Castle,
London, SE1 6SB. Tel: 071 735 8484.
Longlands College of Further Education, Douglas Street, Middlesbrough,
Cleveland, TS4 2JW. Tel: 0642 248351.
Loughborough College of Art and Design, Radmoor, Loughborough,
LE11 3BT. Tel: 0509 261515.
Loughton College of Further Education, Borders Lane, Loughton, LG10
3SA. Tel: 081 508 8311.
Lowestoft College, St. Peter's Street, Lowestoft, NE32 2NB.
Tel: 0502 83521.
Lurgan College of Further Education, Kitchen Hill, Lurgan, Co. Armagh,
BT66 6AZ. Tel: 0762 326135.
Maidstone College of Art and Design (Kent Institute), Oakwood
Park, Oakwood Road, Maidstone, ME16 8AG.
Tel: 0622 57286.
Manchester Polytechnic, All Saints, Manchester, M15 6BH.
Tel: 061 228 6171.
Matthew Boulton College, Sherlock Street, Birmingham, B5 7DB.
Tel: 021 440 2681.
Medway College of Art and Design (Kent Institute), Fort Pitt, Rochester,
ME16 8AG. Tel: 0634 830022.
Middlesex Polytechnic, Trent Park, Cockfosters Road, Barnet, EN4 0PT.
Tel: 081 368 1299.
Mid-Cheshire College of Further Education, Hartford Campus,
Northwich, CW8 1LJ. Tel: 0606 75281.
Mid-Warwickshire College of Further Education, Warwick New Road,
Leamington Spa, CV32 5JE. Tel: 0926 311711.
Monkwearmouth College of Further Education, Swan Street, Sunderland,
SR5 1EB. Tel: 091 548 7119.
Montgomery College of Further Education, Llanidloes Road, Newtown,
SY16 1BE. Tel: 0686 622722.
Napier Polytechnic Edinburgh, Colinton Road, Edinburgh, EH10 5DT.
Tel: 031 444 2266.

Nene College, Moulton Park, Northampton, NN2 7AL.
Tel: 0604 715000.
Newcastle upon Tyne College of Arts and Technology, Maple Terrace,
Newcastle upon Tyne, NE4 7SA. Tel: 091 273 8866.
Newcastle upon Tyne Polytechnic, Ellison Building, Ellison Place,
Newcastle upon Tyne, NE1 8ST. Tel: 091 232 6002.
Newcastle-under-Lyme College, Liverpool Road, Newcastle, ST5 2DF.
Tel: 0782 611531.
Newham Community College, High Street South, East Ham, London, E6
4ER. Tel: 081 472 1480.
Norfolk College of Art and Design, St. George Street, Norwich, Norfolk,
NR3 1BB. Tel: 0603 610561.
Northbrook College of Design and Technology, Littlehampton Road,
Goring-by-Sea, Worthing, Sussex, BN12 6NU. Tel: 0903 830057.
North Cheshire College, Padgate Campus, Fearnhead Lane, Fearnhead,
Warrington, WA2 0DB. Tel: 0925 814343.
North Devon College, Sticklepath, Barnstaple, EX31 2BQ.
Tel: 0271 45291.
North-East London Polytechnic, Romford Road, London, E15 4LZ.
Tel: 081 590 7722.
North-East Surrey College of Technology, Reigate Road, Ewell, KT17
3DS. Tel: 081 394 1731.
North London Polytechnic, Holloway Road, London, N7 8DB.
Tel: 071 607 2789.
North-East Wales Institute of Higher Education, Plas Coch, Mold Road,
Wrexham, LL11 2AW. Tel: 0978 290666.
North-East Worcestershire College, Redditch Campus, Peakman Street,
Redditch, B98 8DW. Tel: 0527 63607.
North Essex School of Art, Church Lane, Braintree, CM7 5SN.
Tel: 0376 21711.
North Lindsey College of Technology, Kingsway, Scunthorpe, DN17 1AJ.
Tel: 0724 281111.
North London College, 444 Camden Road, London, N7 0SP.
Tel: 071 609 9981.
North Oxfordshire Technical College and School of Art, Broughton Road,
Banbury, OX16 9QA. Tel: 0295 52221.
North Manchester College, Crescent Road, Crumpsall, Greater
Manchester, M8 6UF. Tel: 061 740 1491.
North Staffordshire Polytechnic, College Road, Stoke-on-Trent, ST4
2DE. Tel: 0782 744531.
North West College of Technology, Strand Road, Londonderry, BT48
7BY. Tel: 0504 266711.
Norton College, Dyce Lane, Sheffield, S8 8BR. Tel: 0742 372741.
Northumberland College of Arts and Technology, College Road,
Ashington, Northumberland, NE63 9RG. Tel: 0670 813248.
North Warwickshire College of Technology and Art, Hinckley Road,
Nuneaton, CV11 6BH. Tel: 0203 349321.

North East Worcestershire College, Bromsgrove Campus, School Drive, Bromsgrove, B60 1PQ. Tel: 0527 79500.

Norfolk College of Art and Design, St. George Street, Norwich, NR3 1BB. Tel: 0603 610561.

Oxford Polytechnic, Headington, Oxford, OX3 0BP. Tel: 0865 741111.

Oxford College of Further Education, Oxpens Road, Oxford, OX1 1SA. Tel: 0865 245871.

Paddington College, 25 Paddington Green, London, W2 1NB. Tel: 071 723 8826.

Parkwood Tertiary College, Shirecliffe Road, Sheffield, S5 8XZ. Tel: 0742 768301.

Percival Whitley College of Further Education, Francis Street, Halifax, HX1 3UZ. Tel: 0422 58221.

Plymouth College of Art and Design, Tavistock Place, Plymouth, PL4 8AT. Tel: 0752 221312.

Plymouth Polytechnic, Drake Circus, Plymouth, PL4 8AA. Tel: 0752 221312.

Pontypool College, Blaendare Road, Pontypool, Gwent, NP4 5YE. Tel: 0495 555141.

Portsmouth College of Art, Design and Further Education, Winston Churchill Avenue, Portsmouth, PO1 2DJ. Tel: 0705 826435.

Portsmouth Polytechnic, Museum Road, Portsmouth, PO1 2QQ. Tel: 0705 827681.

Ravensbourne College of Art and Design, Kensington Gore, London, SW7 2EU. Tel: 071 584 5020.

Ravensbourne College of Design and Communication, Walden Road, Chislehurst, Kent, BR7 5SN. Tel: 01 468 7071.

Redbridge Technical College, Little Heath, Romford, RM6 4XT. Tel: 081 599 5231.

Richmond upon Thames College, Egerton Road, Twickenham, Middlesex, TW2 7SJ. Tel: 081 892 6656.

Robert Gordon's Institute of Technology, Schoolhill, Aberdeen, AB9 1FR. Tel: 0224 633611.

Rochdale College of Arts and Design, St. Mary's Gate, Rochdale, OL12 6RY. Tel: 0706 345346.

Rotherham College of Arts and Technology, Eastwood Lane, Rotherham, S65 1EC. Tel: 0709 822760.

Royal Forest of Dean College, College Road, Cinderford, Gloucestershire, GL14 2JY. Tel: 0594 22191.

Rycotewood College, Priest End, Thame, OX9 2AF. Tel: 0844 212501.

Rupert Stanley College of Further Education, Tower Street, Belfast, BT5 4FH. Tel: 0232 452111.

Salford College of Technology, Frederick Road, Salford, M6 6PU. Tel: 061 736 6541.

Salisbury College of Art, Southampton Road, Salisbury, SP1 2LW. Tel: 0722 23711.

Sandwell College of Further and Higher Education, Kendrick Street, Wednesbury, WS10 0PE. Tel: 021 569 4592.

St. Martin's School of Art (London Institute), 107 Charing Cross Road, London, WC2H 0DU. Tel: 071 437 0611.

Scarborough Technical College, Lady Edith's Drive, Scarborough, YO12 5RN. Tel: 0723 372105.

Scottish College of Textiles, Netherdale, Galashiels, TD1 3HF. Tel: 0896 3351.

Sheffield City Polytechnic, Pond Street, Sheffield, S1 1WB. Tel: 0742 720911.

Shrewsbury College of Arts and Technology, London Road, Shrewsbury, SY2 6PR. Tel: 0743 231544.

Solihull College of Technology, Blossomfield Road, Solihull, B91 1SB. Tel: 021 705 6376.

Somerset College of Arts and Technology, Wellington Road, Taunton, TA1 5AX. Tel: 0823 283403.

Southampton Institute of Higher Education, East Part Terrace, Southampton, SO9 4WW. Tel: 0703 229381.

Southampton Technical College, St Mary Street, Southampton, SO9 4WX. Tel: 0703 63522.

South Bank Polytechnic, Borough Road, London, SE1 0AA. Tel: 071 928 8989.

South Devon College of Arts and Technology, Newton Road, Torquay, TQ2 5BY. Tel: 0803 213242.

Southend College of Technology, Carnarvon Road, Southend-on-Sea, SS2 6LS. Tel: 0702 432205.

South Fields College of Further Education, Aylestone Road, Leicester, LE2 7LW. Tel: 0533 541818.

Southgate Technical College, High Street, London, N14 6BS. Tel: 081 886 6521.

South Glamorgan Institute of Higher Education, Western Avenue, Llandaff, Cardiff, CF5 2YB. Tel: 0222 551111.

South Nottinghamshire College of Further Education, Greythorn Drive, West Bridgeford, Nottinghamshire, NG2 7GA. Tel: 0602 812125.

South Manchester Community College, Fielden Park Centre, Barlow Moor Road, West Didsbury, Greater Manchester, M20 8PQ. Tel: 061 434 4821.

Southport College of Art and Technology, Mornington Road, Southport, PR9 0TT. Tel: 0704 42411.

South Thames College, Wandsworth High Street, London, SW18 2PP. Tel: 081 870 2241.

South Tyneside College, St. George's Avenue, South Shields, Tyne and Wear, NE34 6ET. Tel: 091 456 0403.

Southwark College, The Cut, London, SE1 8LE. Tel: 071 928 9561.

Stafford College of Further Education, Earl Street, Stafford, ST16 2QR. Tel: 0785 42361.

Index